Specialisation and choice in urban education

From their announcement in 1986, city technology colleges (CTCs) have been presented both as a new choice of school for the inner city and as pointing the way to a more diversified education system. This account of their development uses interviews with key architects of the initiative to identify more clearly the objectives CTCs were designed to serve. It then draws on interviews and observation in CTCs themselves to discover how far these schools are becoming centres of innovation in school management, curriculum and approaches to teaching and learning.

The authors also consider how CTCs have managed the task of selecting intakes representative of their catchment areas, and explore their impact on local schools. Throughout, the CTC policy is considered in the context of the Government's broader political project to challenge 'welfarism' and to encourage entrepreneurship, competition and choice. This report on the experiment comes at a time when a new Education Act, claiming to promote diversity and choice within the system, is offering other schools the opportunity to become more like the CTC model.

Geoff Whitty is Professor of Sociology of Education at the Institute of Education, University of London; **Tony Edwards** is Professor of Education at the University of Newcastle upon Tyne; **Sharon Gewirtz** is Research Officer at the Centre for Educational Studies, King's College London.

Specialisation and choice in urban education

The city technology college experiment

Geoff Whitty, Tony Edwards and Sharon Gewirtz

London and New York

First published 1993
by Routledge
11 New Fetter Lane, London EC4P 4EE

Simultaneously published in the USA and Canada
by Routledge
29 West 35th Street, New York, NY 10001

Typeset in Baskerville by J&L Composition Ltd, Filey,
North Yorkshire
Printed and bound in Great Britain by
Biddles Ltd, Guildford and King's Lynn

British Library Cataloguing in Publication Data
A catalogue record for this book is available from the
British Library

Library of Congress Cataloging in Publication Data
has been applied for

ISBN 0–415–08527–6

Contents

List of figures and tables

Acknowledgements

The research on which this book is based was made possible by a grant from the Economic and Social Research Council (C00232462), and by supplementary grants from the University of Newcastle upon Tyne and from Goldsmiths' College, University of London. Henry Miller and Geoffrey Walford of Aston University were formally associated with the ESRC-funded part of the study, their detailed investigation of Kingshurst CTC being carried out on our behalf. Geoffrey Walford generously provided further information after that investigation was formally over. Roger Dale, formerly of the Open University and now at the University of Auckland, advised us on relevant aspects of the Technical and Vocational Education Initiative and offered some valuable additional insights into the nature of the CTC programme. In addition, we collaborated with Ian Abbott, now at Warwick University but previously at Sunderland Polytechnic, who is conducting case-study research on one CTC's impact on LEA provision. We are also grateful to Michael Adler, Stephen Ball, Richard Bowe, John Fitz, David Halpin, Sally Power and Anne West for a series of discussions which helped us to relate the CTC programme to other recent policy initiatives.

Most of all, we would like to thank the many people who agreed to be interviewed for our study, only a small minority of whom are explicitly identified in the text. We are also indebted to the schools that agreed to our visits. Given the controversy surrounding the CTC programme, and the close scrutiny to which it was being subjected throughout the period of our research, we are especially grateful to those working in the CTCs and at the CTC Trust for their openness to our inquiries.

Chapter 1

City technology colleges: the concept and the context

City technology colleges (CTCs) were first announced at the 1986 Conservative Party Conference. That conference was intended to display a government shaping its programme for a third successive term in office with its radical energies undiminished and with education now high on its policy agenda. Asked that summer what the education system would be like if she were to be re-elected, the Prime Minister (Margaret Thatcher) had turned immediately to the misdeeds of 'left-wing' councils and the consequent need to establish, 'particularly in inner-cities, alternative schools to those the local authorities are running' (*Guardian* 10 July 1986). The canvassing of 'alternatives' from the Right of the party had included the state funding of schools outside local educational authority (LEA) control, and more radical proposals for schools to be run by 'individual trusts' so that they could be shaped and controlled by consumer demand (Hillgate Group 1986). Kenneth Baker's first conference speech as Secretary of State for Education and Science was therefore expected to announce strong measures against the LEAs' alleged monopoly, and so get underway a vigorous pre-election campaign for educational reform as a centrepiece in the party's programme.

Although he avoided any reference to vouchers, the favourite neo-liberal mechanism for creating an open market in education, his main message was a promise to create conditions in which

> Education can no longer be led by the producers – by the academic theorists, the administrators or even the teachers' unions. Education must be shaped by the users, by what is good for the individual child and what hopes are held by their parents.
>
> (*The Times* 8 October 1986)

These had become familiar themes in Conservative policy discourse, without having produced as yet any large steps in that direction. The creation of a 'pilot network' of twenty new secondary schools, to be called city technology colleges, was therefore given an enthusiastic welcome, both as a bold initiative in itself and as an indication of bolder measures to come.

THE CTC PROSPECTUS

In keeping with the enterprise culture, the promotional brochure which the Department of Education and Science (DES) sent out to launch the initiative had the appearance of a City prospectus, complete with a CTC logo (DES 1986).[1] CTCs were to offer 'a new choice of school' to parents in urban areas, 'including the disadvantaged inner-cities', where the 'range and quality' of education was seen to be most in need of improvement. The brochure included a map showing twenty-six 'possible locations' for the new 'colleges', mainly in the industrial conurbations. CTCs would constitute a new category of school – state-funded but independently run – which Mrs Thatcher came to call 'state-independent schools'. They would be run by independent trusts, be free from any LEA control, and embody a unique partnership between government and business. Promoters (later known as sponsors) would 'meet all or a substantial part of the capital costs' (DES 1986: 8), but the Secretary of State would 'pay the CTCs' running costs in accordance with the number of pupils, at a level of assistance per pupil comparable with what is provided by LEAs for maintained schools serving similar catchment areas' (DES 1986: 6). The new schools were to be run by governing bodies which were to employ the staff and be 'free to negotiate pay and conditions of service'. Furthermore, teachers would not necessarily have to have qualified teacher status and governors would be 'free to decide on staffing levels and on the balance between teaching and non-teaching staff'.

Because their funding depended on how many pupils they attracted, CTCs would be provided with an incentive to respond to consumer demand; their independent status, including their ability to hire and fire staff, would give them a certain capacity to respond. At the same time, however, their independence was to be constrained in two crucial ways. Most obviously, their curriculum emphasis had been pre-defined to give them a strong technological, scientific and practical bias:

> CTCs will offer a curriculum in line with the Government's policy for setting high standards in the maintained sector. There will be a large technical and practical element within the broad and balanced curriculum which the Government advocates for all pupils up to the age of 16. The importance of doing and understanding as well as knowing will be emphasised throughout.
>
> (DES 1986: 7)

The promotional brochure included an 'illustrative' version of such a curriculum, which is examined in chapter 5.

The other major constraint on CTCs was to be on their admissions policies:

> CTCs will be required, as a condition of grant, to aim at admitting pupils spanning the full range of ability represented in the catchment area. Pupils will be selected by the Head and the Governing Body on the basis of their general aptitude, for example as reflected in their progress and achievements at primary school; on their readiness to take advantage of the type of education offered in CTCs; and on their parents' commitment to full-time education and training up to the age of 18, to the distinctive characteristics of the CTC curriculum, and to the ethos of the CTC. . . . [E]ducation in a CTC will demand considerable effort from pupils and from their parents. A prime consideration in the selection of pupils will be whether they are likely to benefit from what the CTC offers. All will have some of the positive qualities which will help them succeed.
>
> (DES 1986: 5)

This second constraint seemed to be an attempt to privilege particular kinds of children and parents: it meant that CTCs would not be a new choice for *all* inner-city children, but only for a particular subset of them. Not only would they have to live within a pre-defined catchment area, but also they would have to have the requisite aptitude, commitment and capacity to benefit from a CTC education. They would also have to have parents with the right sort of motivation to make an application in the first place and who could subsequently demonstrate at an interview their commitment to their children's education up to the age of 18. Yet CTCs were also expected to be 'fully representative' of the community they served.

Given so many novel features of CTCs, commentators were quick to read great significance into an initiative of apparently modest scope. Baker's announcement was judged by *The Times* (8 October) to have 'unveiled a school revolution'. Having initially described it as 'the centrepiece of a new deal' (8 October), the *Guardian* then described the hostility which greeted it as 'a row over symbols rather than reality' (20 October). But symbols may contribute powerfully to the construction of reality. If commentators were indeed over-reacting to a 'drop in the ocean of British education' (as the *Guardian* put it), they were certainly encouraged to do so by the way in in which the 'pilot network' was initially promoted and publicised. As Kenneth Baker told the Confederation of British Industry's (CBI) Education and Training Committee a few days after his conference speech, the careful targeting of resources on his new schools would point the way to what could be achieved once the LEA monopoly was broken:

> it will be one of my objectives to ensure that the experience of CTCs is widely shared and widely used. . . . CTCs will not be islands of excellence, set in splendid isolation. They must be lights for others to follow. In this way we shall enrich the whole of the public education system.

This notion of CTCs as a prototype for reshaping the entire system appears repeatedly in contemporary reactions. They were described, for example, as 'cuckoos in the nest' of public education (O'Connor 1986); as 'the spearhead of Tory hopes of resurrecting a semi-independent sector of schooling' (*Financial Times* 27 February 1987); as embodying a return to academic selection and a divisive differentiation between types of school (Simon 1987); and as 'part of a clearly-defined New Right strategy to destroy the state system of schooling as we know it and hand education over to the control of crude market forces' (Chitty 1987: 67).

It is certainly possible to see in the CTC policy an attempt to encourage a 'quasi-market' in education. Many of its features prefigured those that were subsequently to be embodied in the Educational Reform Act 1988 which in turn put CTCs on a statutory basis. That Act contained the same apparent contradiction between devolution and constraint that characterised the CTC initiative. On the one hand, it extended some of the market-oriented characteristics of the CTC programme to other schools. All schools were to be given the incentive and a certain capacity to be more responsive to consumers via per capita funding and local management. A new sector of grant-maintained schools was introduced which, like CTCs, were to be independent of LEAs, funded by the central government and to which parents had to apply directly. In addition, open enrolment meant that parents could apply to schools outside their immediate neighbourhood – ironically leaving CTCs as the only schools with tightly controlled catchment areas. On the other hand, the introduction of a National Curriculum, together with national testing at ages 7, 11, 14 and 16, severely limited the extent to which schools could respond to market forces if the market were to demand other than what the government felt should be on offer.

THE CONTEXT OF THE INITIATIVE

Whatever the educational arguments for or against CTCs and the Education Reform Act, it would be naive to regard either of them as a narrowly educational initiative. In reading the policy discourse that surrounded the launch of the CTC programme in 1986, it seems clear that it was positioned within several policy sets that were becoming central to the Thatcher government's overall strategy. That government's explicit commitment to common policies across different policy areas has served to reduce the relative autonomy of education policy and made it easier to demonstrate a relationship between education initiatives and other favoured projects (Dale 1990; Edwards *et al.* 1992a). In the case of CTCs, these included government strategies for restructuring the workforce, for controlling the inner city, and for replacing planned provision of welfare with market-oriented provision. Thus, in seeking to make sense of the origins and the contradictions of the CTC policy, it is important to recognise its relationship to the broader economic, political and cultural projects being pursued by the Thatcher government as it prepared for and entered its third term of office.

The economic project

The CTC initiative was partly justified – or legitimated – as the product of a wider concern, that the education system was not meeting the needs of the economy. Five months before the launch of CTCs, Cyril Taylor, who was later to play a leading role in the CTC initiative, had published a pamphlet reporting the outcomes of a conference held by the Centre for Policy Studies, a leading right-wing think-tank. One of those outcomes was a call for 'the setting up of 100 technical secondary schools funded by central government on a direct grant basis' which would help to meet what Taylor (1986) identified as 'the crucial need to improve training and vocational education' and to rectify the damage done by the comprehensive system:

> Are secondary schools . . . failing our nation? More and more people think so. The egalitarian ideals of comprehensive schools have not been translated into the provision of a trained workforce. Mixed ability teaching has meant that the half of the school population more interested in vocational training than in academic education have been inadequately catered for. That vocational skills are so little taught has to a large degree been responsible for young British school leavers finding it so hard to obtain work. For a whole lost generation little or no training investment has been made. No wonder we have lagged behind our industrial competitors.
>
> (Taylor 1986: 24)

Taylor welcomed the existing Youth Training Scheme and Technical and Vocational Education Initiative as steps in the right direction, but argued that they were not enough because secondary schools were still not 'providing relevant education for the half of their pupils who do not desire a purely "academic" curriculum'.

There are two broad strands to the economically grounded critique of the British education system. The first is that it continues to be permeated by anti-industrial and antientrepreneurial attitudes. This is the so-called British Disease which was supposedly caused by an anachronistic commitment to the classical literary curriculum of the Coleridgean and Arnoldian tradition (Mathieson and Bernbaum 1988) and, according to Corelli Barnett, by the welfare state. Welfarism, Barnett wrote, had produced 'a segregated, sub-literate, unskilled, unhealthy and institutionalised proletariat hanging on the nipple of state maternalism' (Barnett 1986: 304).

The other strand is the concern that the British education system is failing to produce a labour force appropriate for a changing world economic climate characterised by the inter-nationalisation of production. The concern of British industrialists here is that, because labour is so cheap in other regions of the world, particularly those bordering the Pacific, Britain needs to ensure that a significant proportion of its labour force is highly skilled. The perceived problem is succinctly diagnosed in a CBI document, *Business in Education*:

> Britain will continue to have to compete internationally more on quality and 'added value' than on price. The UK is a relatively high cost source of labour, when compared with the Pacific Basin, for instance, *where skilled workers are likely to be paid in the order of £25 a week, even when operating world-class capital equipment*; . . . this makes it all the more important that the vocational education and training systems encourage and develop the abilities needed for product innovation, product quality, high level diagnostic skills and so forth.
>
> (Confederation of British Industry 1988: 28, emphasis in original)

The vocational education and training systems are also seen to need to produce an adaptable workforce because of the unpre-dictability of the skill-demands generated by technology-driven growth. There is the added problem of the 'demographic time bomb'. Between 1986 and 1994 the number of 16- to 17-year olds in the UK will have fallen by more than a quarter, from just over 1.7 million to just under 1.25 million. In some areas the shrinkage will be greater, with the inner cities expected to experience the largest reduction in school-leavers. Taken together, the demographic factor and changes in the nature of the production process threaten employers with a situation in which – 'The [labour] market could switch fairly quickly from one favouring "buyers" to one where the "sellers" have the upper hand' (CBI 1988: 28). The problem of high unit labour costs resulting from the skills shortage may be exacerbated by employers adopting a short-term perspective – offering high wages to attract under-trained 16- and 17-year-old school-leavers to meet immediate production needs. This possibility has led to calls for the creation of a norm 'where full-time employment does not begin until the age of 18 unless it is combined with training' (CBI 1988: 30).

Although CTCs clearly fit well into such a context, there is justifiable scepticism about how far a pilot programme of CTCs can produce the sorts of economic changes being demanded. However, as we note in subsequent chapters, it is possible to understand CTCs as a largely symbolic response to the skills problem or as a catalyst designed to produce changes in the system as a whole. It is also important to see CTCs as part of a political as well as an economic project for the inner-city.

The political project

At 3.30 a.m. on election night in June 1987, Margaret Thatcher was to stand on the steps of Conservative Central Office and tell her supporters:

> on Monday, you know, we've got a big job to do in some of those inner cities, a really big job. Our policies were geared – education and housing – to help people in the inner cities to get more choice and politically, we must get right back in there because we want them too, next time.
>
> (cited in Hennessy 1990: 696)

Her mission for the third term, as she defined it in an interview with Peter Jenkins (*The Independent* 14 September 1987), was to extend the 'Thatcher Revolution' to the inner cities. A crucial aspect of this 'revolution' was the assault on the power base of the Labour Party at municipal level. Thatcher's showdown with Ken Livingstone had already resulted in the abolition of the Greater London Council. The 'Torification' of the remaining Labour-controlled metropolitan boroughs was to be achieved partly via the poll tax (community charge) and the proliferation of urban development corporations. The transfer of more local authority housing to the private sector, and a restructured education system were central elements of this project. The government was assisted in its 'mission' by the tabloid press which was already engaged in promoting the idea of the 'loony Left' Labour council. Education was a central target in this press campaign, with anti-racist, anti-sexist and anti-heterosexist teaching identified as the main examples of what the *Sun* once called 'barmy burgherism'.

Much of Baker's speech to the 1986 Conservative Party Conference in which he first announced the CTC policy had consisted of just this kind of tabloid rhetoric:

> Just reflect for a moment what would happen to education under Labour. Last week in Labour Brent a Conservative councillor, when an interview with a black candidate was running two hours late, looked at her watch and shuffled her papers. She was accused of 'racist body language'. . . . This is the sort of pressure that parents, governors, teachers and Conservative councillors have to face all the time. It's nothing to do with education. It is bigotry masquerading as freedom.
>
> (*The Times* 8 October 1986)

In the pamphlet arising from the Centre for Policy Studies conference mentioned earlier, Cyril Taylor had recognised the role that new schools might play in winning popular support for the Conservative Party. Referring to the proposal for directly funded technical schools to be initially 'concentrated in deprived inner city areas', he wrote:

> This recommendation is perhaps the most important to come out of the conference. Its implementation would prove that the Conservative Party cares about education for the non-academically minded majority of school children – in much the same way as the sale of council housing proved that the Party cared about home ownership for all.
>
> (Taylor 1986: 30)

Here Taylor drew the same parallel between education reforms and the sale of council houses that Mrs Thatcher was to make fourteen months later:

> Just as we gained political support in the last election from people who had acquired their own homes and shares, so we shall secure still further our political base in 1991–2 – by giving people a real say in education and housing.
>
> (interview, *The Independent* 7 September 1987)

Like the 'right-to-buy' policy and the expansion of share owner-ship, CTCs may thus be viewed as a means of giving working-class voters in Labour and marginal areas a 'stake in Toryism'. It has been suggested that the proposed locations for CTCs, listed in the DES brochure which launched the initiative, were chosen with that aim in mind. McLeod has noted that, while some of the proposed sites were subject to exceptional unemployment levels and structural economic changes, 'other motives cannot be ruled out entirely' and that 'there was before the election a concentration of marginal parliamentary constituencies in certain of the towns specified'. Such a concentration was most pronounced in Leicester and Nottingham, but also existed elsewhere in the Midlands and in Bristol, Portsmouth, Norwich, Newcastle and Bradford (McLeod 1988: 77, 82).

Thus CTCs were apparently seen as a vote winner and, despite the controversy that has surrounded them, it would seem that they continue to be viewed in this way. The vote-winning potential of CTCs was noted by Michael Ashcroft, the chairman of the security company ADT which donated £1 million to the Wandsworth CTC. In a letter to Sir Paul Beresford, leader of Wandsworth council in January 1990, he wrote that the CTC would 'no doubt be of much help to your local Conservative candidates for the May 1990 elections' (cited in *Guardian* 21 May 1991). Although Baker's successors as Secretary of State have sometimes seemed lukewarm towards CTCs, the initiative was given renewed impetus in July 1991 in anticipation of an earlier general election than actually occurred. John Major, who had succeeded Mrs Thatcher as Prime Minister, made a renewed attack on the Left's 'mania for equality' and announced a package of education policies which included a big expansion of the CTC programme (*Daily Telegraph* 4 July 1991).

The socio-cultural project

Whether or not CTCs offered immediate electoral advantages to the Conservative Party, they can be seen as part of a broader attempt to cultivate values more conducive to a market system of welfare provision. They were certainly seen as a way of developing 'the qualities of enterprise, self-reliance and responsibility which young people need for adult life and work and for citizenship' (DES 1986: 4). The fact that they were to be run by industrial sponsors was particularly conducive to the cultivation of such qualities. Indeed as we shall see in chapter 3, for some of the sponsors, that was a major attraction.

The task was not only to encourage members of a market society to think of themselves as individuals competing against other individuals in order to maximise their own interests; they also needed to be encouraged to accept that it was appropriate for there to be winners and losers in the system. Acceptance of these consequences could be promoted by the cultivation of two values – family responsibility and self-reliance. The motivational admissions criterion for CTCs is particularly relevant here, in that this in itself may be seen to constitute a mechanism for the promotion of market values. As Roger Dale has put it, a CTC place for one's child

> is the reward for parental commitment to family self-improvement, initiative and deservingness. It is a reward for those whose commitment both the grammar school (because of its single (ability) basis of selection) and the comprehensive school (because of its commitment to egalitarianism and universalism) left unrewarded.
>
> (Dale 1990: 14)

It was also important for cultural, as well as structural, reasons to wrest schools from the control of labour municipalities that were seen to be promoting the 'wrong' values in schools. Thus, for example, Baker's 1986 conference speech included an attack on the Inner London Education Authority (ILEA) for its attitude towards competition in schools and in school sport. But CTCs not only were the first step towards the removal of schools from LEA control, and hence from supposedly anti-market influences, but also represented a significant attack on the teacher unions. Although de-unionisation was not something made explicit in the initial publicity, few of the CTCs have recognised unions for purposes of negotiation.

Not surprisingly, then, many aspects of the CTC policy resonate clearly with a number of key themes of broader Conservative policy discourse under Margaret Thatcher and John Major. As we shall see, this has had significant consequences for the implementation of the policy, though it has not determined, in any straightforward manner, the ways in which the CTCs themselves have developed.

THE NATURE OF THE RESEARCH

Our own decision to undertake research on the CTC initiative derived from a specific interest in the changing focus of education policy under the Thatcher government and a more general concern with processes of policy formulation and implementation. Edwards and Whitty had just completed (with John Fitz) an evaluation of the Thatcher government's first educational initiative, the Assisted Places Scheme (Fitz *et al.* 1986). That scheme had been attacked from the outset as a government-sponsored withdrawal of support from maintained schools, and as indicating an intended return to academic selection. But its promotion largely as a traditional ladder of opportunity for 'able children from less well-off homes' meant that it had only limited appeal for radical advocates of parental choice. Among our conclusions, five years after its introduction, were that it could not be significantly expanded on its own terms, and that it had yet to be followed by any of the 'logical' next steps towards privatisation which had been confidently predicted (Fitz *et al.* 1986). The 1986 CTC announcement could be seen as a significant next step, and our research proposal to the Economic and Social Research Council (ESRC) emphasised continuity with the earlier study of assisted places in its approach to policy analysis.

We wanted again to follow a controversial initiative through from the deliberations of policy-makers to the experiences of some of those directly affected, combining a wide-ranging analysis of its antecedents and origins with detailed investigation of its implementation. During the course of the research, we interviewed those most often identified as the initiative's political architects, of whom only Lord Griffiths declined to be seen; DES officials and relevant HMI; the chairman and the chief executive of the CTC Trust; 'lead' sponsors and representatives of actual or potential sponsoring firms; project directors and education advisers for particular CTCs; and the principals of most of them. We discussed resistance to the CTC programme with representatives of companies which refused the government's invitation to sponsor CTCs, with chief education officers and other LEA staff in authorities directly affected by the creation of a CTC, with heads of 'competing' secondary schools in CTC catchment areas, and with teachers and parents who had campaigned against the conversion of an existing school into a CTC. We explored the experiences of staff, pupils and parents in CTCs and in some nearby comprehensive schools. Altogether, we carried out almost 400 interviews, as shown in Table 1.1. In drawing on these interviews later in the book, we have identified by name only those politicians or other public figures whose general views on the CTC programme are already a matter of public record.

Table 1.1 Number of interviews by category

Politicians/political advisers	7
DES/HMI	5
CTC Trust	4
Business and industry	18
Local anti-CTC campaigners	4
LEA officers	13
CTC project directors/education advisers	8
CTC principals	13
Headteachers of schools in CTC catchment areas	14
Teaching and support staff	41
Students in CTCs and neighbouring comprehensive schools	199
Parents of students in CTCs and neighbouring comprehensive schools	65
Other	5
Total	396

Encouraged by the ESRC to extend the scope of the research to include possible influences on government thinking of 'lessons' learned from elsewhere, we also made three study visits to the United States to examine the development of 'magnet' schools and of more recent reforms in urban secondary education, and tried to assess the relevance of Germany's apparent success in giving high status to technologically oriented secondary education.[2] This part of the study involved nearly fifty additional interviews.

As in most research projects, plan and practice diverged considerably. The result, as reflected in this book, is much more an account of the origins of CTCs and their significance as an item of government policy than a series of case studies of the kind which Geoffrey Walford and Henry Miller (1991) made of Kingshurst CTC in Solihull. Although, from time to time, we do draw upon case study material (including some of that provided for us by Walford and Miller), we make no attempt to assess the educational success or failure of particular CTCs. Any such educational judgements must be premature at a stage in their development when none has been open for more than four years or has its full intake of students.

What is of interest to us, however, is the way in which claims about their success and failure are already being used to legitimate new policy initiatives. As early as 1990, an enthusiast (and trustee of Djanogly CTC in Nottingham) was already claiming that, although the CTC initiative 'must be given time to yield its lessons', it had already shown that 'good education is most likely to be practised where there is diversity of provision, wide parental choice, and open competition between schools' (Regan 1990: 43). Then, when the then Secretary of State (Kenneth Clarke) referred to the 'very encouraging progress' CTCs had made (CTC Trust 1991a: 3), and the 1992 White Paper describes them as 'excellent' (Department for Education 1992: 4), the only 'evidence' for such assertions was their popularity with parents and a consequent level of consumer demand which has embarrassed the suppliers. We do not share the government's assumption that popularity necessarily demonstrates quality, especially where the schools concerned are still establishing their niche in the market and parental perceptions of them range as widely as our own evidence suggests. Their claims only serve to reinforce our view that CTCs need to be understood as part of a much broader project on the part of the Thatcher and Major governments.

THE SCOPE OF THE BOOK

Our account of the origins of the CTC policy which follows in chapter 2 is an attempt to explain why it was announced in that form at that time. While keeping in mind the broader context discussed earlier, the emphasis here is on the CTC policy itself rather than its relationship to other policy agendas. In moving on to look at the implementation of the policy, we tried to balance national and local evidence so as to avoid remaining too much within the original policy-makers' frame of reference. If the hubris of policy-makers is often the nemesis of those charged with carrying the policy out (Fullan 1991), then those working to establish the pilot network have had to confront obstacles overlooked or underestimated when the target of twenty CTCs by 1990 was first announced. The adaptations which resistance to the programme has enforced are described in chapter 3.

Chapter 4 explores one of the most controversial aspects of CTCs, their recruitment policy and the impact that their existence is having on patterns of parental choice. Although those working within the CTC 'movement' were notably open and co-operative, given the hostility which often surrounded their efforts and the close scrutiny to which they have been subjected,[3] the faltering progress of the programme limited the amount of data we were able to gather in this context. Because of the nature of the initiative and the small numbers of pupils entering CTCs during the period of our research, it would have been inappropriate to aggregate our intake data on a national basis. This is therefore one part of the book where we provide data about specific CTCs and the experiences of pupils and parents applying to them.

Delays in an initiative which was ill thought out and poorly planned made it impossible to gather as much evidence about the actual working methods of individual CTCs as we wished. However, even though this limited the number of visits it proved feasible to make, our account of the innovativeness of CTCs in chapter 5 is based on extensive interviewing, both within the CTC 'movement' and outside it. But, although we also observed over forty lessons in six CTCs, together with various 'extension' and 'enrichment' activities, these observations make no claim to be representative. Indeed, many of our visits focused explicitly on what CTC staff saw themselves as being able to do, or do more easily, than would have been possible in the maintained schools from which almost all had been recruited. The nature and scope of innovation, always intended to be a main theme in the study, was given greater prominence as the CTCs' own rhetoric of presentation came to emphasise their importance as 'centres of research and development', a role with which they seem markedly more comfortable than they are with acting as a Trojan horse planted in the midst of maintained secondary education.

As we saw earlier, even within a framework of education policy, the CTC programme was soon overtaken by and absorbed into that wholesale restructuring of the education system promoted by the Education Reform Act 1988. This fact alone has made it impossible to assess with any clarity the effect of CTCs on schools around them, and the account in chapter 6 of the impact of CTCs on local provision is necessarily tentative. It is also the case that the particular evidence we draw from south-east London may not be a guide to the impact of CTCs elsewhere. There is no doubt, however, that in addition to providing 'fresh opportunities' to some children in urban areas – thereby creating another 'ladder of opportunity' to be judged (from an individualist perpective) by the benefits to those who climb it – CTCs were intended from the outset to have powerful exemplary effects. It seems from our evidence that their role as 'beacons' has proved problematic and that their function as prototypes has been complicated by uncertainty about what they are supposed to typify. Even so, CTCs were certainly promoted and perceived as piloting a radical restructuring of the education system in terms of greater specialisation, diversity and choice, concepts that have recently served as the main props of a White Paper's 'new framework for schools' (DFE 1992).

In our final chapter, we return to the broad policy contexts within which CTCs can be located and their emergence explained. We suggest that, in some ways, the idea we encountered among critics that they are merely an abomination of Thatcherism is too limiting. However, while pointing out that CTCs need to be understood in relation to other educational and social changes, not only in Britain but also in many other parts of the world, we also question whether the CTC policy is quite as 'mould-breaking' as it appears. Although the rhetoric of CTCs and related policies trades powerfully on a variety of assumptions about the emergence of a new social order, the reality looks like being all too familiar.

Chapter 2

The emergence of city technology colleges

That the CTC programme was seen from the outset as piloting more radical, more extensive reforms makes it difficult to identify its primary purposes. The title of this book emphasises its role in enhancing consumer choice in a more specialised and competitive educational market. While that has been prominent in the rhetoric surrounding CTCs, uncertainty about the initiative's main thrust broadened its appeal by allowing various interest groups to see opportunities for advancing their particular concerns.

In this chapter, we try to explain why CTCs appeared when they did as 'a new choice of school'. The account is complicated because while their imputed 'architects' are not numerous, they seem to belong to policy-forming networks with rather different objectives and very different priorities. As with the sudden announcement of the Technical and Vocational Education Initiative (TVEI) in November 1982, 'unique, secret and personal origins . . . make it hard to identify sources with any precision' (Dale *et al*. 1990: 13). In focusing on the more directly traceable sources, we have also taken account of its more loosely connected antecedents. CTCs were a direct expression of a political preference for schools which would be independent of local authorities and so freed to find their place in the market. But they can also be seen as yet another attempt to give a technically oriented secondary education something like parity of esteem, and to provide an alternative (and modernised) version of the 'ladder of opportunity' from the inner cities which had traditionally led through the grammar schools. We begin, however, with an obvious if superficial explanation for their announcement in October 1986 – that they were largely a personal initiative by a new, ambitious Secretary of State eager to make his mark early and to emphasise a change in that office from introspection to action.

INITIATORS OF THE CTC PROGRAMME

It is clear that Kenneth Baker identified strongly with what he called 'my network of new schools in urban areas', and that he took a proprietorial interest in its creation which neither of his immediate successors maintained. Where his own predecessor had been a seeker after profound remedies for educational ills, prepared (indeed inclined) to agonise over finding them, Baker was 'the supreme pragmatist ... more easily seduced by the superficially attractive'.[1] He had replaced Joseph in May 1986 to bring less agonising and more action to a department already being prepared for an unprecedented period of radical interventionism. His approach, as defined by one of his senior civil servants, was – 'let us press on, let us make things happen' (cited in Ball 1990: 181).

As an early demonstration of making things happen, the CTC programme had obvious attractions. It overtly challenged the LEA 'monopoly', but on a manageably small scale for a department entirely unused to creating or running schools. It also did so at what was (wrongly) assumed would be modest cost to the Treasury. The schools would be conspicuously modern, their high technology appearance being readily associated with Baker's reputation as the minister who put computers into schools in 1981, shortly after taking responsibility for Information Technology (IT) within the Department of Trade and Industry. They could be presented as doing something for inner-city areas at a time when the government was beginning to publicise its commitment to urban regeneration; as displaying traditional Conservative support for ladders of educational opportunity; and as a step towards broadening parental choice which would have far more appeal to the party's market advocates than the Assisted Places Scheme because it was not confined to parents of academically able children. CTCs also embodied a unique partnership between business, industry and government in rejuvenating the school system.

All these themes were touched on by Kenneth Baker in his conference announcement, and in his subsequent publicising of the initiative. That so much was supposed to be achieved so quickly demonstrated – as he told the CBI's Education and Training Committee on 14 October 1986 – that 'this is not a do-nothing government' but a government committed to vigorous action. Considerable personal responsibility can be attributed to Baker for the form which that action took. When we interviewed him after he had left the Department of Education and Science for the Home Office, he gave the impression of a reforming minister who had to make his own reform agenda. At the time of his appointment, he claimed that he had

> found very little which could be described as worked up anywhere in the whole range of educational performance. . . . There'd been various vague ideas about technical schools, but you could not say they'd been worked out in any shape or form to any degree.

In that area of policy-making, and despite his own involvement in launching TVEI, his predecessor bore him out. For while Lord Joseph thought CTCs an excellent idea, he was adamant in claiming no credit for them. He could not recollect the idea being pursued during his time at the DES, though there had been some pressure from Bob Dunn (then Schools Minister) for something resembling magnet schools.

There had also been general pressures in that direction. Particularly prominent had been the New Right campaigning for the creation of new direct-grant schools, sometimes with an explicit emphasis on inner cities and sometimes with a bias towards technical education. Thus Bob Dunn was credited in late 1985 with a specific proposal to create sixteen to twenty 'technical schools in main urban centres', outside LEA control and 'funded directly by the taxpayer via a national education trust', for which pupils would be selected who could benefit from a special emphasis on 'sciences, business studies, and computer programming'. Dunn's motives were identified as those of giving parents more choice, aiding bright working-class children, and encouraging schools to specialise (*Sunday Times* 22 December 1985). In January 1986, as we noted in chapter 1, a conference initiated by Cyril Taylor on behalf of the right-wing Centre for Policy Studies recommended the creation of '100 technical secondary schools funded by central government on a direct grant basis'. These would be concentrated initially in 'deprived inner-city areas' and then extended to every LEA to act as 'beacons' for other secondary schools (Taylor 1986: 2, 30). Looking back on that conference four years later, Sir Cyril Taylor described it to us as 'one of the principal starts' of the CTC programme, and the published report of its outcomes as having 'started the ball rolling'. There was, he said,

> a clear feeling from the fifty leading industrialists present that comprehensive secondary education, especially in urban areas, simply wasn't delivering the skills that they needed. And it was also their view that the poor outcomes was what was creating high unemployment, high youth unemployment. It wasn't necessarily the lack of jobs, it was the lack of skills.

Within the DES itself, although not (in Baker's phrase) 'worked up', a briefing paper prepared late in 1985 by Bob Dunn and Stuart Sexton (Joseph's political adviser) proposed the creation of new, directly government-funded schools. Even as an outline proposal, however, there was a significant difference in emphasis between its authors. Stuart Sexton described it to us as having emerged from discussions about devolved budgets and locally managed schools which were already underway before Baker took office. Sexton himself wished to see new schools which would be within the state system but 'in conformity with the way we were now thinking – directly funded on a per capita basis'.

> Certainly we cashed in on the fashion for using the word technology. . . . You see, there are two themes running in parallel here. There's the belief of people like me that schools would be better if they could run their own shows so you've got pressure towards self-governing schools funded on a clear basis of running their own budget. That's one principle. Then added to that as far as CTCs are concerned is – let them be showpieces for how technology can be taught. . . . To me, the pressure for policy change was very much towards self-managing schools and freedom from political and financial control. And the market. And the belief that if you could only free up the system so that schools were free to respond to the market and had an incentive to do so – namely, that their funding depended on it – then all these questions about the

National Curriculum and more technology or less would sort themselves out because they'd be responding to the market.

According to Sexton, it was Dunn who had argued that the new schools should have an overt emphasis on technology and that they should act as 'catalysts' in this respect as well as in their per capita funding. Dunn himself confirmed that he had been interested in 'that side rather than the idea of direct-grant status'. Indeed, he recalled having originally wanted to

> steer LEAs into opening schools like that. We would say – 'Right, Buckinghamshire, North Yorkshire, Manchester, we feel that you should establish a technological school in your local authority to act as beacons of light'. And I felt then that there'd be industrial involvement and people would be seconded from firms to argue and debate and teach marketing, economic and industrial practices and that sort of thing and then – that was my original thought – the policy came out as these things do, partly from Number Ten, partly from Kenneth Baker, that it was funded from industry itself. . . . But I'm happy with the way it turned out.

Dunn saw a vital curriculum gap to be filled and a new choice to be offered, the choice of being 'educated in the new technology'. He described how he had taken the idea to Sir Keith Joseph, who 'after a long debate decided not to proceed with it'. After Baker's appointment, he had thought – 'let's try this idea again, dusted it off, updated it slightly'.

As indicated in Dunn's earlier comment, the most significant 'updating' seems to have come from Baker himself. Instead of complete government funding on a per capita basis as Sexton wanted, or financial incentives to LEAs to develop specialised technology schools as Dunn wanted, the policy initiative emerged not only in more innovative but also in more vulnerable form. The notion of private sponsorship was described to us by Sir Cyril Taylor as 'Kenneth Baker's crucial input', a reflection of his belief that it 'wouldn't do any good substituting central bureaucracy for local bureaucracy' and that this could be avoided by creating 'a direct relation between local employers and their schools'. As Baker himself explained it, sponsorship would display a unique commitment of business and industry to an educational programme. In practice, as we show in chapter

3, the difficulties of keeping to an ambitious timetable for creating twenty CTCs were greatly increased by the reluctance of major companies to make this particular 'long term investment in the adult and working population' (DES 1986: 6). But Baker's larger ambition was to break into what he saw as a closed world badly in need of fresh ideas. If a wish to 'infuse into the education system more of a technological thrust' was one of the 'threads' which came together in the CTC programme, the other was a wish to diversify a system which was too 'monolithic' and resistant to change.

> You had this huge continent of state education, and you had this much smaller island of private education – 500,000 pupils, quite a large island actually and an island which had a great creaming effect. And there was a great gap between the two, and a great gulf. . . . And I always thought it was very unfair that parents who could not afford to send their children to private schools didn't have a wider choice of schools themselves. In many areas of the country, it would come down to your local comprehensive and 'that's it, folks'.

Thus the provision of greater variety and choice represented the other impetus behind the CTC programme.

We now explore those main 'threads' in more detail. Asked by us whether he had given greater priority to one than to the other, Baker replied:

> No. I felt that I had to inject as much energy and points of creative energy into the system as I could. If I'd just tried to reform the existing system, then I think that my fate would have been the fate of any reformer of the education system – namely, sinking into the bog.

It is to that intention of disturbing the system that we turn.

CREATING COMPETITION AND CHOICE

It is easy to understand why the CTC programme was so widely seen as foreshadowing more substantial challenges to LEA provision. Announced during a strong attack at the Conservative Party Conference on the sacrifice of consumer choice to producer interests, it was soon being described by the Secretary of State as the first source of real competition within the state system since

1902 and as a prototype for how that entire system might be remodelled.[2]

Some form of direct challenge to LEAs had been expected as the political campaign against them gathered pace. The Prime Minister's antipathy towards them was well known, and the head of her Policy Unit at that time (Brian Griffiths) was credited with a strong belief that education would be much the better for being subjected to the free play of supply and demand. Also credited with a major influence on Conservative preparations for the 1987 election, which clearly included giving priority to radical educational reforms, he has been identified in that ideological context as a 'main architect' of CTCs.[3] If he was, then it was their potential for opening up the system rather than their character as technology schools which constituted their appeal. Certainly a small but well-publicised spearheading project had obvious attractions at a time when a full frontal assault on LEAs was still slightly premature.

The ideological ground-clearing for that main assault had been thorough and systematic. Its beginnings are traceable to the founding in 1957 of the Institute of Economic Affairs (IEA), dedicated to promoting study of the market as the most effective 'device for registering individual preferences and allocating resources to satisfy them' (Harris and Seldon 1979: 5). At that time, protestations of belief in the market were cries against the wind. Even when the first Black Papers were published in 1969, their largely conservationist 'reappraisal of progressive assumptions' was both attacked and defended as a deliberately heretical departure from the orthodoxy of the time. In the early collections, choice and diversity were portrayed largely in terms of preserving elite independent schools and grammar schools, and of providing appropriate opportunities for poor but able children to attend them (Edwards et al. 1989: 55–9). Even in that mainly traditionalist context, however, Ralph Harris (later director of the IEA) drew from his experience as a parent campaigning for the preservation of Enfield grammar school the 'larger lesson' that state schools would become properly responsive to their clients only when 'consumer sovereignty rests securely on the power to choose between competing suppliers' (Harris 1969: 71). That became the main theme of what Rhodes Boyson called 'the English Libertarian Right', and it is apparent in the last sets of Black Papers. Establishing the 'true democracy'

of the market-place would make 'popularity with customers . . .
the real test of a school's efficiency'; the founding of new schools
run by educational trusts was to be encouraged, and poor
schools should not be protected from the consequences of
market failure (Boyson 1975: 29; Cox and Boyson 1977: 5; see
also Sexton 1987).

If the function of radicals is to prepare the way for reform by
'questioning the unquestioned and thinking the unthinkable',[4]
then the radical Right had been highly successful by the mid-
1980s in carrying the previously unthinkable into the centre of
educational policy-making. By that time, another right-wing
pressure group was campaigning for all secondary schools to be
run by independent trusts so that they could survive only by
their capacity to attract and satisfy customers free to 'place
their custom where they wish' (Hillgate Group 1986: 7). Its
pamphlets, like those of Stuart Sexton, sometimes present
an uneasy blend of free market and preservationist positions
(Knight 1990: 141–2). But to Sexton, whose directorship of the
IEA's Education Unit gave him a conspicuous platform, the
ideal education system consisted entirely of 'self-governing, self-
managing schools obliged for survival to respond to the market'.
It was an objective which made him well disposed to any
intermediate steps – 'vouchers, direct-grant schools or whatever'
– which could constitute 'irreversible improvements in that
direction' (Sexton 1986; 1987: 8–10). The strategy was to be
both incremental and tactically varied, which was how some
critics also perceived it (Pring 1987). Where Baker defended
CTCs as a deliberately disturbing influence within the state
system, Sexton saw them as 'self-managing' schools which would
be the model for all.

To those who regarded the existing system as unacceptably
monolithic, any move towards greater diversity was welcome;
but the CTC programme had some particular attractions. The
combination of public funding with 'independent' status which
led Baker to describe them as 'half-way houses' between public
and private education was useful in blurring the boundary
between the two sectors. It was a combination with an obvious
resemblance to the 'Crown schools' energetically canvassed shortly
before the CTC announcement, but the CTC formula was
more radical than that. A revival of the direct-grant list had
often figured in New Right campaigning, and was hinted at

several times by the Prime Minister herself in 1985–6.[5] But simply reopening the old list would have been a conservative, even reactionary, measure if it meant no more than readmitting a hundred or so grammar schools to their former intermediate status. What the New Right wanted were new schools not only freed from LEA control, but also free from central government interference since its criticisms of producer interests extended to DES officials.[6] It was a bias to which was attributed the failure of educational vouchers to gain acceptance as being practical as well as ideologically attractive (Seldon 1986). From that perspective, it was an added attraction of CTCs that they were to be 'owned (or leased) and run' by their promoters.

It was for that reason that *Education* predicted a significant moment in long battle when Baker announced 'the funding of twenty high technology schools', because the party's right-wingers and left-wingers would be 'watching the wording with unusual care' (3 October 1986). The right-wingers were to be disappointed that a fine opportunity for piloting their favourite funding mechanism – the voucher – had again been missed, Baker clearly preferring to retain possibilities of blending his new schools into the maintained system. We commented earlier that the Assisted Places Scheme was largely irrelevant to the 'libertarian' Right as long as its overtly academic frame of reference limited its extension of choice to parents of academically able children. Yet an assisted place could be described as 'a kind of voucher' (West 1982) in so far as it represented earmarked purchasing power at a school which the parent had chosen (provided, of course, that the school had felt able to choose the child). An expansion of the scheme to cover other kinds of schools and a wide range of pupil ability could therefore be advocated (as it was by Stuart Sexton) as one of the incremental steps towards a more open system. Offering free places to pupils who were 'representative' of the catchment area both socially and in ability, CTCs were to receive for each of them a grant 'sufficient to meet all items of current expenditure which would fall on an LEA for one of its own schools' (DES 1986: 8). That grant could be regarded as being, in effect, an educational voucher for the duration of a distinctive form of secondary schooling. But from a 'pure' neo-liberal perspective, a voucher 'in effect' was still not a voucher in fact because the government would still be meeting CTCs' recurrent costs. Sexton's tactical response to that objection was to emphasise how a combination of measures like the creation of CTCs, opting out, open enrolment and local management of schools (LMS) were creating the necessary conditions for an open market without the upheavals which a voucher system would create.

We have concentrated so far on pressures to break up a system of secondary education regarded as being structurally too uniform, and we explore in chapter 5 the extent to which CTCs represent a 'new model' in organisation and management as well as in their funding. But it was also argued on the Right that 'monopoly' provision had suppressed consumer demand in relation to the content of schooling, and had allowed schools to descend towards a common mediocrity. As Bob Dunn put the point to us:

> There's too much blandness in 11–18 provision, there's too much sameness, it's too general, it doesn't bite enough. And if you get *The Times* of yesterday a week ago you'll find a letter from me arguing for extra funding for which schools can bid to develop a specialism like science or languages or maths, and then they can act as a beacon of light.

That notion of a curriculum more differentiated between schools and types of schools had become a strong theme in policy discussions. If a revival of separate grammar schools was not yet practical, and there were sections of the Right which argued strongly that it was, then schools which remained comprehensive in intake should be encouraged to specialise in what they taught. Thus Rhodes Boyson had urged all comprehensives to offer extra tuition in at least one area of the curriculum, and had proposed specialist 'centres of excellence' which could be 'maths, science, computer studies, technical, trade, industrial, humanities, classics, business, even sport schools'.[7] In a pamphlet published by the Centre for Policy Studies, Fred Naylor (1985: 5–6) argued against 'common secondary schooling', his particular advocacy of a 'special programme in support of technical schools' being placed in the context of general support for 'schools of specialized character'. It was from a similar perspective that the *Financial Times* saw in the CTC programme 'a reversal of the comprehensive movement by providing more specialized secondary education to those with appropriate aptitudes' (27 February 1987).

Although itself biased towards technology, the 'CTC concept' was clearly capable of being extended to other kinds of curriculum specialisation (Hillgate Group 1987: 39), and so appeared to resemble in this respect the 'magnet' schools of the United States. Indeed, Stuart Sexton's introduction to an IEA pamphlet extolling this US model of curriculum diversity refers to CTCs explicitly as 'a kind of technology magnet' challenging the notion of the 'common' school (Cooper 1987: 1). Since they were to be located in urban, mainly inner-city locations, and were required to recruit intakes 'representative of the communities they serve', they might also seem similarly intended to exert a 'magnetic' pull across traditional boundaries of race and class. But as we suggest, later, the comparison is misleading. As an explanation of the origins of CTCs, it is simply wrong. If Kenneth Baker indeed 'dropped in to the Bronx High School of Science' and saw it as 'just the sort of specialized high school that could give a competitive boost to the rest of the system' (Rowan 1988), he did so almost a year later than his CTC announcement. Regan (1990: 19) is able to identify magnet schools as 'a second source' of CTCs (after TVEI) only by mistiming Baker's US visit, and treating it as an easy step to 'apply in the British context' the establishing of schools with a 'special excellence in technical and vocational education'. Sir Cyril Taylor was later to describe the 'magnetising' of all secondary schools as a 'logical extension of the CTC concept' (Taylor 1990: 12). It would be more accurate, however, to say that the most conspicuous magnet schools, like the Bronx High School for Science, for example, are high status and highly selective, and that they bear considerably more resemblance to direct-grant grammar schools than to the new-style specialised comprehensives which CTCs were supposed to become.

CTCs were also unlike magnet schools in representing what was at that time a very un-American form of conspicuous curriculum intervention by central government. In that respect, they pose a dilemma for the Right. For believers in education as a commodity to be shaped entirely by market forces, such intervention had to be questionable – whatever advantages Stuart Sexton (for example) saw in 'cashing in on the fashion for using the word technology'. From their perspective, government prescription of what schools should teach was incompatible with freeing educational provision to follow consumer demand. As defined in 1986, however, the CTCs were to offer a very particular form of specialisation, the 'large technical and practical element' within their curriculum requiring that they would be 'unusually directive' about what pupils should study (DES 1986: 7). We turn now to the justification offered for that government intervention.

CURRICULUM SPECIALISATION AND THE PROMOTION OF TECHNOLOGY

Their character as 'technology schools' or 'inner-city forcing houses for science' caught the attention when CTCs were first announced (*New Scientist* 16 October 1986: 23). It is from that perspective that McCulloch (1989a; 1989b) portrays them as an old rather than a new choice of school – as the latest in a long line of attempts to establish a strong technical strand in secondary education, give it the resources and status necessary to remedy past neglect, and thereby counter the channelling of children into traditionally academic forms of curriculum. While McCulloch recognises that their main purpose 'may have been other than to promote technical education' (1989b:49), it is in that context that he criticises the government's apparent disregard of historical lessons when launching the initiative. In particular, he argues, reference to the 'usable past' should have indicated the importance of clearly identifying what the CTCs were intended to achieve, deciding whether they were primarily to train technicians or a technological elite, and justifying why a small network of separate schools was preferable to incorporating a 'strong technological element' throughout secondary education.

During our interviews with them, Kenneth Baker, Bob Dunn and Cyril Taylor all regretted the demise of secondary technical schools. Baker attributed their 'early death' to egalitarian objections to 'segregating children into horny-handed sons of toil' for whom technical training was appropriate, and to a foolishly egalitarian belief that everyone was capable of benefiting from 'a grammar school education'. Dunn described himself as pleased to represent a constituency (Dartford) which still had two of the 'five or six technical schools left in the country', with another two 'next door in Bexley'. He even identified explicitly as 'historical' the main source of his own proposal to create a

new network of technologically oriented schools, a proposal
which he saw as restoring something of the diversity in secondary
education which had been intended in 1944. Identifying the
German *Realschule* as a significant model for CTCs, Taylor
explained the German post-war system as following the English
tripartite pattern and regretted that the 'comprehensive school
ethic had washed out not only grammar schools but the hundred
and sixty or so technical schools which had done such a good
job'.

   Despite these examples of wishing to return to distinct types
of schools, McCulloch's question about why a small network of
CTCs was preferred to permeation has obvious relevance to the
Technical and Vocational Education Initiative launched only
four years earlier. Although some commentators have traced
CTCs back to that source, continuity with the earlier initiative –
the largest direct intervention in the school curriculum attempted
by a British government – is hard to establish. Initial DES
promotion of CTCs certainly refers to 'building on the lessons
of TVEI', but it neither identifies what those lessons were nor
explains why they needed to be built upon. Yet by the summer
of 1986, some 65,000 pupils were involved in TVEI schemes in
600 schools and colleges. David Young's announcement in July
(as Secretary of State for Employment) that the initiative would
now be extended to all secondary schools could therefore be
defended as a natural extension of its scope. Even though the
results of various evaluations were still awaited, Young argued
at his press conference that the government was unwilling to
delay when TVEI had already achieved such 'obvious' success
in developing a more practical, more economically relevant,
approach to secondary education. If that were so, it only
highlights questions about why another and intensively targeted
intervention was thought necessary and requires a brief outline
of the political and educational objectives of the earlier initiative.

   In claiming credit for having launched TVEI in November
1982, David Young (then chairman of the Manpower Services
Commission) describes it not inaccurately as his 'dawn raid on
education' (Young 1990: 89). It was planned well away from the
DES, so that only Sir Keith Joseph among the Education
ministers had been involved in the decision and only the
Permanent Secretary among DES officials had been even fore-
warned. The announcement was made in the Commons by the

Prime Minister herself, presenting it as a stimulus to technical and vocational education through the development of a 'distinct curriculum', and it was Norman Tebbit's Department of Employment which took responsibility for the initiative – thereby rousing DES officials to protest to Keith Joseph at 'selling his birthright to the dreaded MSC' (Young 1990: 89).

From a structural perspective it can be seen as a deliberately disturbing intervention in the self-controlled and largely self-contained world of education, with the reliance on LEAs bidding for contracts from the MSC a mechanism for avoiding the usual 'capture' of educational initiatives by the 'producers' (Dale *et al.* 1990: 4). Young presented it that way both in his memoirs and when we interviewed him shortly after their publication. But he also combined human capital arguments for reskilling the workforce with frequent references to the power of a 'practical' approach to motivate pupils likely to be untouched by conventionally 'academic' study. In this, he drew his inspiration less from the technical high schools of France and Germany than from the work of the international Organisation for Rehabilitation through Training (ORT), which had been founded in St Petersburg in 1880 to promote the economic integration of Jewish people through providing them with the technical skills to gain employment in the towns. Becoming international after the Revolution, it has had its headquarters successively in Berlin, Paris, Geneva and then (from 1979) in London. Especially prominent in Israel, it claims to influence secondary schooling in fifty countries and the nature of that influence was firmly defined when we interviewed its director-general (Joseph Harmatz) and education director (Dr Gideon Meyer) in October 1990. Far from being 'crazy about technology', a claim often made by critics, they insisted that ORT was committed to technologically oriented but general secondary education, and to using modern technology across the curriculum to facilitate active learning and so motivate the otherwise unmotivated. This seems to have been Young's view too. He had been ORT's British chairman, and regarded his involvement in its European programme as a qualification for running TVEI (interviewed in *Education* 19 November 1982).[8] While he approved of ORT's success in promoting technical schools of high status, he was even more impressed with that focus on vocational preparation which seemed to him to permeate Israeli secondary schools of all kinds. It was this aspect of ORT's work which he claimed to have urged on Joseph, Tebbit, Peter Morrison (then Parliamentary Secretary at the Department of Employment) and Kenneth Baker at several briefing sessions in ORT's London office during the summer and early autumn of 1982. It is an aspect which raises questions about the target group at which TVEI was primarily directed which reappear in relation to CTCs and to which we return.

It is the method by which Young initially proposed to launch TVEI which provides the most direct link with the CTC programme. For what he suggested to Sir Keith Joseph was a 'series of technical schools around the country' which, if they were successful, would beneficially 'infect the system'. As 'no other secretary of state would have done' in response to such a proposal, Young told us, Joseph 'sat and thought about it for a moment, and then just said yes'.

Young was then able to persuade the Prime Minister that through a 'happy accident' of sloppy drafting, the 1973 legislation establishing the MSC had also given it the authority to run its own schools and that this power should be used if LEAs refused to co-operate (Young 1990: 89; Ainley and Corney 1990: 51–2). He also talked of industrial backing for such schools (*Education* 19 November 1982). But although the prospect of ten or more newly created 'Young schools' was thought at the time to have considerable appeal to a notably self-confident minister, and though it is tempting to see in his overt references to that possibility an early expression of government preference for breaking the LEA monopoly, he argued in his book and in our interview that they were primarily a threat to secure LEA co-operation without prolonged, time-wasting negotiations. The threat was real enough, because several apprenticeship training institutions had been lined up as possibilities for recruiting intakes of two hundred and fifty 14 year olds for a four-year programme combining a 'normal education' with 'technical and vocational subjects'. But while the possibility that LEAs would resist the temptation to bid for money to run the pilot projects had to be considered, his declared preference (reinforced for its own reasons by the DES) was to 'persuade the existing system to run our new programme, provided that we retained control in its entirety' because full LEA involvement would greatly increase the chances of the 'TVEI approach' permeating schools (Young 1990: 93).

Strong residues of that view were apparent when we interviewed him about the origins of CTCs. Although the Cable and Wireless Company of which he was chairman had recently announced its joint sponsorship (with the Wolfson Foundation) of a CTC in Bristol, he described himself as having been critical initially of the extent to which the pilot project had been 'outside the main system' and so made vulnerable to being 'shunted aside as irrelevant'. It is also significant that, although he had been Secretary of State for Employment in 1986, he seems not to have been involved in preparing the CTC initiative and to have been among the ranks of the surprised when it was announced. Nor do we see any independent evidence to support Joseph Harmatz's claim that the CTC programme as well as TVEI had been 'born' in ORT's London office. Young's own wish to see large numbers of technologically oriented schools made him much better disposed to plans to extend the initiative by encouraging voluntary-aided and opted-out schools to adopt or adapt the CTC model.

Although designed to challenge the educational 'establishment', the CTC initiative had the attraction from a DES perspective of being under its own supervision. From the market perspective outlined in the previous section – and Young himself was firmly in support of letting schools make their own decisions and live with the consequences – CTCs had the advantage of being outside the maintained system. But what of their status as technology schools? In that respect, did they represent a 'logical next step' by turning a TVEI strand within schools into a curriculum orientation for entire schools (Regan 1990)? And what might be achieved by promoting technical education in such a specialised way, in contrast to the permeation model of curriculum innovation which TVEI represented? That question raises other familiar questions about the ability, attitudes and occupational destinations of the pupils for whom a technically oriented version of secondary education was thought to be especially suitable.

The advocacy of separate technical schools in two pamphlets published by the Centre for Policy Studies (CPS) gave priority both to the poor quality of the British labour force at technician level – drawing heavily on the research of Prais and Wagner (1986) in doing so – and to the motivating effects on low-attaining pupils of a more 'practical' curriculum (Naylor 1985; Taylor 1986). Although Naylor also regretted the failure of the former technical schools to compete with the grammar schools for 'really able pupils', his approval of the *Realschulen* rested mainly on their success in providing, and for a larger proportion of the age-group than went to the more academic *Gymnasien*, high-level skills for those 'entering semi-professional occupations at technician level' (Naylor 1985: 56). The logical conclusion of his analysis was therefore a call for a substantial extension of technical education rather than a thin topsoil of high-status 'technology schools'. Similarly, the 1986 CPS conference on employment recommended the establishing of 'up to a hundred' direct-grant technical schools as a direct contribution to solving severe skills shortages at 'technician' level. But it was also careful not to portray those schools as modernised grammar schools. By catering for 'the half of the school population more interested in vocational training than in academic education', a Conservative Party traditionally preoccupied with provision for the most gifted would at last demonstrate its concern for 'those of our young people who would prefer to acquire commercial and technical skills' (Taylor 1986: 24, 27).

We consider in chapter 4 whether early predictions are being fulfilled that CTCs would be 'subsidized grammar schools in high technology clothes' (Glazier 1986). The evidence suggests that they were not intended to rival the kind of traditional academic education which the Assisted Places Scheme had sponsored, and that their principal architects were more influenced by a conviction similar to Keith Joseph's that many children were being alienated by a secondary curriculum which seemed remote and irrelevant. Thus Kenneth Baker, in the interview cited previously, claimed to have been looking not to a revival of 'workshop-type schools', but to a demonstration of how 'you could reawaken the interest of children' across a wide range of ability through 'good teaching of technology' using all the resources of 'the micro-chip generation'. It was to be an important part of the CTC 'mission' to raise staying-on rates far above the deplorably low levels evident in many inner-city areas, and especially among those whom Baker described to the CBI's Education and Training Committee (14 October 1986) as regarding 'their last two or three years at school as a sentence to be served, not as a crucial period of preparation'.

It is much easier to see how CTCs could be 'beacons' in that respect than to see a small 'pilot network' making a significant contribution to the 'economic project' described in our opening chapter. We return to the function of modernising the work-force when discussing in chapter 3 why support for CTCs from business and industry was so much less than the government had expected. Even within a more limited frame of reference, unanswered questions about continuity with TVEI also apply to other initiatives within the maintained sector which had at least some of the same objectives and of which mention might have been made in 1986 if only to explain why more radical or more targeted moves in the same direction were now thought necessary. For example, the schools-into-industry project (SCIP) had achieved some success in establishing working contacts (Jamieson 1986; Shilling 1987), a 1988 CBI survey reporting that the majority of secondary schools now had direct links with some local companies (the proportion of companies which had links with schools being significantly lower). The London Compact was well advanced in 1986, involving direct business sponsorship of pupils willing to work hard, attend well, and stay on. In a particularly close parallel, and in direct competition for private money, the 'Education 2000' project involving all six Letchworth secondary schools had similar origins in concern at pupils' alienation from schooling, schools' remoteness from the 'real' world and their resistance to change, and a commitment to using new technology to enhance the 'art of learning' (Fisher 1990).

We consider in later chapters the extent to which CTCs are becoming a new kind of school, and can be seen as promoting forms of school organisation, curriculum and teaching not found in the main system. Of the policy strands which came together in the 'pilot network' announced in 1986, it is hard not to see those educational objectives as subsidiary to the main political purpose of challenging the LEA 'monopoly' and pointing the way to a restructuring of the entire system. From that perspective, it was an initiative which the government could not allow to fail. We turn now to how a small-scale but ideologically significant programme was implemented, and how and why it was so strenuously resisted.

Chapter 3

Resistance and adaptation

Despite a high-profile announcement and glossy promotion, the CTC programme was preceded neither by careful planning nor by any assurance that constituencies essential to its success were already implicated. David Young's 'dawn raid on education' in 1982 had also been a considerable surprise. But whereas TVEI was to be entirely publicly funded, the creation of CTCs depended not only on the goodwill of business and industry but also on a willingness to make 'substantial' contributions to their capital costs. It was therefore a serious tactical error not to have recruited sponsors whose names could be announced almost immediately so as to give the project momentum. The DES map of twenty-six 'possible locations' for CTCs also suggested a national network with its points in all the main conurbations and no part of the country unduly favoured. In practice, the difficulty of finding sponsors was compounded by the difficulty of finding sites, and intensified by the even greater difficulty of finding sponsors in the 'right' areas and sites in areas where there were sponsors. The network which has emerged therefore differs significantly from what was envisaged in 1986, and reflects some tactical ingenuity (see Table 3.1).

Thus the clustering of CTCs in south London is explained by friendly LEAs, a co-operative diocesan authority, and a merchant company with its 'own' school. There is a CTC in Gateshead rather than in Newcastle because the site of a redundant Catholic secondary school was made available, and no CTC in Liverpool because there was no Church co-operation to offset the council's hostility. After scouting several possibilities, Stanley Kalms (chairman of Dixon's) found the northern site he wanted when the Conservatives briefly gained control at Bradford. The

Table 3.1 The intended and actual locations of CTCs

DES (1986) listing of 'possible locations'	Actual CTCs	Projects proposed but not implemented
Newcastle/Gateshead	Emmanuel, Gateshead	
Sunderland		
Middlesbrough (north central)	Macmillan, Middlesbrough	
Bradford	Dixon's, Bradford	
Leeds, Chapeltown		
Hull		
Preston		Preston
Knowsley		Sefton
Liverpool		Liverpool
Manchester, Moss Side		Manchester
		Trafford
Nottingham	Djanogly, Nottingham	
Derby	Landau Forte, Derby	
Wolverhampton		
Sandwell		
Birmingham, Handsworth	Kingshurst, Solihull	
		Walsall
	Thomas Telford, Telford	
Leicester, Highfields		
Coventry		
Norwich		Lincoln
	Brooke, Corby	
Bristol, St Paul's	John Cabot, Kingswood	Bristol, South
Plymouth		Plymouth
Portsmouth		
Southampton		
		Brighton
London area		
	Harris, Norwood	
	Performing Arts and Technology, Selhurst	
North Peckham	Haberdashers', New Cross	
	ADT, Wandsworth	Hillingdon
	Bacon's, Bermondsey	Barnet
	Leigh, Dartford	Bexley
Notting Hill		
Hackney		
Newham		

form taken by the pilot network therefore owes more to accident than to planning. Even so, the original timetable of twenty CTCs in operation by September 1990 has had to be revised substantially, as Table 3.2 shows.

Although the CTC Trust raised the total to nineteen by including 'CTCs under consideration in various new forms' (CTC Trust 1991a: 2), plans for only fifteen CTCs have been finalised as we write. To reach even this lower target, more slowly than originally envisaged, has required

Table 3.2 The CTCs and their sponsors

CTC (with opening date)	Main sponsors
Emmanuel, Gateshead (1990)	The Vardy Foundation
Macmillan, Middlesbrough (1989)	BAT Industries plc
	Cameron Hall Developments
	The Davy Corporation plc
	British Steel plc
Dixon's, Bradford (1990)	Dixon's Group
	Haking Wong Enterprises
Djanogly, Nottingham (1989)	Harry Djanogly
Landau Forte, Derby (1992)	The Landau Foundation
	Forte plc
Thomas Telford School (1991)	Mercers' Company
	Tarmac plc
Kingshurst, Solihull (1988)	Hanson plc
	Lucas Industries plc
Brooke, Corby (1991)	Hugh de Capell Brooke
John Cabot, Kingswood (1993)	Cable and Wireless plc
	Wolfson Foundation
Leigh, Dartford (1990)	Sir Geoffrey Leigh
Bacon's Bermondsey (1991)	Southwork Diocesan Board of Education
	Philip and Pauline Harris Charitable Trust
	London Docklands Development Corporation
Harris, Norwood (1990)	Philip and Pauline Harris Charitable Trust
Haberdashers', New Cross (1991)	Haberdashers' Company
Performing Arts and Technology School (1991)	British Record Industry Trust (BMG Records, EMI Records, Polygram UK, Sony Music Entertainment, Virgin Records, Warner Music (UK), Island Records, Telstar Records)
ADT, Wandsworth (1991)	ADT Group plc

considerable modifications to the programme as it was initially proposed.

In this chapter, we trace how the initiative has been implemented, how responses to it have produced significant changes to the original model, and how these in turn have generated new responses and further changes. We concentrate here on the implementation of the programme as a whole, leaving to later chapters a more detailed account of how policy has been translated into practice within the CTCs themselves.

THE SEARCH FOR SPONSORS

Both in his Conservative Party Conference speech and his early promoting of the CTC programme, Kenneth Baker laid claim to a queue of eager backers. Interviewed on *Weekend World* towards the end of the year, he declared himself 'immensely encouraged' by the 'very strong response from industry' (7 December 1986). Yet despite the DES reference to prior discussions with 'individuals and organisations who share the Government's concerns' (DES 1986: 2), there is no evidence of consultation even with interest groups like the CBI, the Industrial Society or the Engineering Council whose support for such an exercise in economically relevant curriculum modernisation might have been expected. Nor had there been consultation with major companies, like ICI and BP, already actively involved in 'partnership' arrangements with schools.

Baker seems to have been surprised that his attempt to sell the initiative to the CBI's Education and Training Committee on 14 October 1986 was not received more enthusiastically. A subsequent private meeting between his junior minister (Angela Rumbold) and a CBI delegation proved even cooler, and produced some sharp questioning about why CTCs were necessary when TVEI had been such a conspicuous success. The meeting was followed by strenuous efforts to enlist support at the highest levels of business and industry. In our interviews with representatives of actual and potential sponsors, there were frequent references to dinners at Downing Street or with the Secretary of State; there were also ministerial letters and phone calls to old acquaintances in the business world, and more formal letters from senior civil servants to local dignatories in likely locations.

Kenneth Baker himself was active in the campaign. As he told us, 'I went out and banged the drum. I talked to industrialists and persuaded them to support the schools, and it wasn't difficult to persuade them quite frankly – they wanted to do it'. The following accounts illustrate both Baker's personal involvement, and the soft approach of relying on personal contacts and the networks which these might activate. A Bristol businessman

> was asked by Kenneth Baker, when he was Minister of Education – I had known him for quite a number of years – whether I would undertake the task in Bristol of trying to get together a team to go ahead, raise money and form a City Technological [sic] College. Now, I can't say I knew a lot about them at the time, but I had a brochure sent down by Kenneth and the project interested me. So, I contacted another old friend . . . and we had a little lunch of the Society of Merchant Venturers, where someone – I forget the name – came down from London to talk to us.

Like many initial approaches, this proved abortive. In contrast, another businessman was successfully recruited by Baker, whom he already knew, while they were on a sponsored walk together.

> He asked me if I would help him with the CTCs as they wanted to develop some in the north-east. I said, 'What are they?' . . . He started to explain to me the reasons why he wanted me to do it and I listened. He made one fundamental statement which I'm holding him to – he said that he wanted these schools to be in inner-city areas for disadvantaged children. He explained that children from the poorer families were not staying on at school, and he gave me reasoned arguments to consider it. I am a great one for competition, I think it's the life blood of our society, and I do believe that the bastions of bureaucracy will have to be challenged . . . and I thought that the idea he had behind the CTCs was good. It would also challenge the existing educational system. . . . We haven't got enough competition, and I felt that CTCs would compete and force the present system, which is good but could be improved, to look at itself. That is why I supported him, basically on the principle that he was trying to help disadvantaged children in inner cities.

He also regarded his sponsorship of a CTC as part of his wider contribution to the regeneration of the region.

Though many were called to help Baker's initiative, few were persuaded to do so as promptly as that. The CBI declined to reinforce the government's efforts, remaining carefully neutral towards an initiative which some of its leading members so evidently disliked, while the line taken by representatives of the Industrial Society was to dismiss CTCs as a diversion from the valuable work already going on in strengthening school–industry links. The government was therefore faced with the potential embarrassment of a political initiative denied support by the very economic interests it was promoted to serve. The consequence was that heavier methods of 'persuasion' were used to complement the soft approach. They were directed especially at such blue chip companies as BP, ICI, IBM, Esso, Unilever, British Telecom and Sainsbury's, from any of which even nominal support would have been valuable. A politician not himself involved in the campaigning seemed to assume that civil servants 'couldn't be directly involved in touting for sponsorship'. Yet we know from interviews with several targets of 'touting' that senior civil servants were so involved, and that their participation was fiercely resented. We also know that some companies were reminded, if they had not already reminded themselves, that government contracts played a significant part in their business, and that some company representatives who advised against participation were subjected to strong personal attack. Such 'arm-twisting', a term used repeatedly in these interviews, seems to have gone beyond anything its victims had experienced before from sources in and around government. In similarly off-the-record comments to Stephen Ball, one industrialist noted his company's vulnerability to ministerial pressure because of its high-tech visibility and its unwillingness to upset important people whose decisions affected 'other things that we do'. Another recalled that his company had been pressed hard because its chairman was a Thatcherite supporter and had been 'screwed on the basis of goodwill to cough up a million pounds and it is not by conviction, it is by what I would term the need for some industrialists to cough up to ensure that Baker doesn't fall flat on his face' (Ball 1990: 118–19). The resistance of major companies might have been less stiff if they had been consulted before the CTC programme was announced, and if the announcement had been less overtly political. As a company representative put it, matters might have been very different if the government had recognised the value of existing industry–school partnerships and sought to build on them; if it had invited industry to co-operate with government in sponsoring a series of careful educational experiments; and if the potential transferability of what might be learned from those experiments had been considered from the start. As it was, the initiative was seen as being 'unfair and divisive'.

It was certainly perceived as being in competition, financially and politically, with existing partnership arrangements with schools and LEAs. Bob Finch, then education liaison officer for ICI, describes himself and his chairman (Sir John Harvey-Jones) as having agreed that whatever other objections there might be, the 'sticking point' was their unwillingness to say to schools with which they had 'built up close and friendly relations over ten or fifteen years' that the company was now going to put £1 million into 'an entirely new school on your patch which will probably recruit some of your best teachers and cream off some of your pupils' in the supposed interests of increased choice and competition (*Times Educational Supplement* 1 February 1991). That loyalty to 'old friends' was certainly appreciated on Teesside, where ICI is the largest employer and was described to us by Cleveland's chief education officer as giving 'tremendous assistance' to schools. Fearing that the limited funds available for non-profit-making activities might be 'siphoned off towards CTCs and all the rest of the schools would lose out', he had been delighted that the company had resisted 'some very high-level arm-twisting'.

Another dilemma confronting national companies was clearly stated by a former executive of a thriving supermarket chain which had continued to refuse sponsorship, though his present company had already decided to back one when he joined it.

> For a national organisation I would seek to put my investment of funding into nationally influential projects. . . . So if I had a choice between putting it all into one specific location or spreading that money, then I would always choose the national route and my biggest objection for a national company on CTCs was that I felt it was an inappropriate strategic placement of a large amount of money. I mean we're talking

big money here. And that money could be and was better spent at a more spread level and at a more national, influential level and therefore I advised [my company] not to become involved.

It also seemed sensible to some companies not to offend the local council in an area where the company was a major employer if that council was firmly opposed to CTCs. That reluctance was sometimes interpreted more generally as a preference among large corporations for doing business with other (albeit public) corporate bodies. Commenting on the predominance of individual entrepreneurs among the early sponsors of CTCs, Kenneth Baker remarked on their 'freer, open-ranging minds' and his frequent experience that when he started talking to a big company – 'I knew I was talking to somebody who preferred to deal with an education authority, they were in the same network!' The CTC Trust's chief executive made a similar comment about affinity in outlook, although she also recognised that the process of reaching a decision about funding might also be more complicated.

> Where the big companies are involved, first they have fairly well developed corporate affairs policies and are fairly well committed, and they like as part of that policy to spread their money around a bit in little dollops here and there. And secondly, the structure of a very large company is not dissimilar from the structure of a local authority or a government department. And their ways of working are not dissimilar, in the sense that people will avoid taking decisions because they have to go through endless boards and committees and endless reports. So that makes it difficult for those companies, however much they say 'What a good idea', to actually put their money where their mouth is.

'Spreading money around' is explicitly the policy of companies like BP, as is a preference for supporting 'mainstream' ventures the benefits of which could be readily diffused through the system. But other companies had different priorities.

In some cases, and where local hostility to the project was not too intense, backing a CTC presented a way of gaining publicity for 'doing good'. Since the promotion of CTCs was thought to have gained something from the example of magnet schools, the

US example of companies using educational sponsorship to enhance their image or counter adverse publicity might also have had some relevance.[1] Thus the promotional brochure inviting sponsorship for Bradford's CTC began by referring to 'a possible new source of skilled staff for your business', then continued by reminding companies of the value of 'good community relations':

> Their investment in community projects can help with recruitment, promote consumer awareness of company products, and form a vital part of a company's social responsibility profile. . . . Benefits for corporate patrons and sponsors are several, and substantial investors will have an opportunity to name facilities and continuing educational services at the CTC. The Trust Fund's charitable status means that convenanted contributions can be tax efficient both for the donor and the Trust.

Such an appeal is more likely to be successful with small companies of the kind heavily represented in the list of over fifty sponsors displayed (for example) in Kingshurst's entrance hall. But a large national company, expanding its interest in a region where it was 'weak as a name', also saw in CTC sponsorship 'part of a package of things that we are doing . . . to improve our image and our positioning in that region. . . . It was another string to the bow, if you like, of what we're doing up there'.

The reservations of some major companies about supporting CTCs clearly carried less weight with individual entrepreneurs, and with some large companies noted for an entrepreneurial style of leadership. The Hanson Trust became the first substantial business sponsor, the *Financial Times* recording its pledge of funding to the first projected CTC in Solihull as a '£1 million boost for the competitive spirit' (25 February 1987). Lucas Industries became a second sponsor, though with a pledge of services rather than money. The trickle of support grew slowly. Press reports pointed out how many early sponsors – for example, Hanson, Lucas, Argyll Stores, Trusthouse Forte, and Harry Djanogly – were significant contributors to Conservative Party funds or (like British American Tobacco) backed right-wing organisations like Aims of Industry and the Centre for Policy Studies.[2] Rumoured offers of future honours for CTC sponsors led one director of education to remark ruefully: 'I can't offer a knighthood for not having a CTC, can I?'

Such apparently partisan support was damaging to the image of the initiative. So was the publicity given to the financial dealings of several sponsors and would-be sponsors. For example, British and Commonwealth Holdings crashed spectacularly when it seemed about to sponsor a CTC in Bristol (subsequently rescued by Lord Young's Cable and Wireless Company) and there was continuing press speculation about the affairs of ADT (and of its Bermuda-based chairman Michael Ashcroft) which switched from backing a CTC project in Barnet to one in Wandsworth because a site was easier to obtain there and it wanted – according to one of its negotiators – 'a fast bang for its bucks' (*Times Educational Supplement* 19 January 1990). More dramatically, the supposed lead sponsor of a 'green', Steiner-oriented CTC in Brighton, Ivor Revere, was accused of acquiring a site through a property company of which he was also a director, and then selling it to the CTC Trust at £200,000 more than he had paid for it without having put up any of his own promised money. John MacGregor admitted in the Commons (24 April 1990) that 'Mr Revere had undertaken to donate £1 million . . . but had withdrawn without having made any payment' and that his 'commission' had been discovered only several months after the sale. Labour's education spokesman Jack Straw criticised the slackness which allowed 'an ostensible donor to become a beneficiary', and called for 'a special independent audit of the CTC Trust and for the suspension meanwhile of the wasteful and disreputable CTC programme' (*The Independent* 2 May 1990). As we show later, there were also persistent claims, in the context of mounting criticism of the proportion of public money going into the programme, that sponsors had promised much more money than they had paid. For some of those sponsors, initial enthusiasm may have been dented by the recession of the early 1990s. At least one of the early sponsors listed in the 1990 *Sunday Times Book of the Rich* (Beresford 1990) had dropped out of the updated list published less than two years later (*Sunday Times* 10 May 1992).

The first wave of CTC sponsorship seems to have depended heavily, then, on the kinds of entrepreneurial companies that were successful in the middle years of the Thatcher government. There is, in contrast, a relative absence of companies which might have enhanced the high-technology, industrial modernisation image of the programme (see Table 3.2). As the programme has progressed, more 'blue chip' companies have offered at least some support. Yet in relation to the preference of many national companies for supporting mainstream initiatives, there is an interesting comparison with the sponsorship of the 'Education 2000' (E2K) project which involved all Letchworth's six secondary schools 1986–9. Placing a similar emphasis on 'modernising' secondary education and on the transforming effects of a high level of information technology (IT) provision, that project (which included the two independent schools) was strongly supported by the Hertfordshire LEA. Of CTCs' 'chief sponsors', only BAT Industries also supported E2K; of CTCs' 129 'supporting sponsors' as listed by the CTC Trust (1991a), only eleven also backed the other project; companies backing E2K but not the CTC programme included Allied Lyons, Barclays Bank, British Aerospace, British Airways, Courtaulds, Digitial Equipment Company, Ferranti, IBM, ICI, Reed International, Unilever and George Wimpey.

We want now to consider more closely the motives of individuals and companies sponsoring CTCs. Certainly the opportunities for direct involvement created by CTCs' freedom from 'corporatist' control seem to have had special attractions for entrepreneurially minded businessmen. Sir Geoffrey Leigh (Dartford), Harry Djanogly (Nottingham), Stanley Kalms (Bradford), Sir Philip Harris (Croydon and Bermondsey), Peter Vardy (Gateshead) and John Hall (Middlesbrough) are prominent examples of strong individual identification both with the CTC ethos and with individual CTCs, and of a lack of concern for avoiding controversy. Thus John Ramsden, the project director at Nottingham, contrasted a major national company's reluctance to offer any support except as an addition to what it contributed to maintained schools with Harry Djanogly's vigorous backing and continuing 'proprietorial' interest. Ramsden described Djanogly as 'anti-corporatist', and as seeing the civil service and bureaucracies generally as 'inimical to individual achievement' – seeing a sharp contrast between bureaucracy and initiative which was drawn by other sponsors we interviewed. Convinced of a steep decline in the quality of recruits to his business, Djanogly had wanted to use his money to repay a 'debt' to his adopted country (his grandfather having emigrated to Mansfield, and started the family clothing business there). A similarly strong sense of regional identification and of repaying 'debts' was apparent in our interviews with John Hall (Middlesbrough) and Peter Vardy (Gateshead). John Hall referred explicitly to 'capitalism with a social conscience' and to businessmen like himself 'putting money back into the community in which we've earned our living', and Peter Vardy to having been 'well blessed by the way the business has developed over the last few years, so it's putting something back into the area'. Both these men have strong local roots, and a strong commitment to 'regenerating' the north-east. Like Harry Djanogly, they were also attracted by a quite unusual opportunity for being directly involved in a school. An initiative described by an executive from one company as being 'too maverick and round-the-edges' to be supported was described by an executive from another as attractive precisely because it was 'different', and because it allowed 'people like ourselves from the private sector to be . . . much more actively involved in the provision of education than had hitherto been the case . . . and to make a direct input'.

Alongside the generalisations we have suggested, there are also differences between sponsors which illustrate the openness of a loosely defined project to a variety of objectives. Such differences appear even in relation to the 'surer preparation for working life' which CTCs were intended to provide. Some sponsors have seen an opportunity to intervene directly in the local labour market so as to improve the supply of skills and attitudes directly relevant to their business. Others expressed a more general anxiety, of the kind discussed in chapter 2, about the inability of the existing education system to provide the necessary skills and attitudes. Thus a leading retail company was described by one of its executives as wanting to 'increase the knowledge of both pupils and teachers about retail as a career because there is this nonsense that . . . retail is a corner shop and is rather a simple business'. It had supported a CTC partly to improve that image. A director of an industrial firm explained its support for the local CTC as arising from the persistent neglect of manufacturing industry in careers evenings at local schools, and a belief that the CTC would be different:

The final straw was when I went to one where there were sixty participants, and only three of us made anything. . . .

We felt that both schools and the careers service were actively encouraging people to go into white-collar work.

Though reflecting a belief that conventional secondary schooling had failed, such views also reflect rather different conceptions of the 'output' which a CTC might produce and so of its appropriate intake. While some actual or potential sponsors envisaged CTCs as picking out children who were 'trainable' – and what was implied by that seemed to be white, able and aspiring working class – others appeared to favour a more comprehensive intake and a wider range of destinations. Furthermore, conceptions of output ranged from a generally higher 'standard' of school-leavers broadly prepared for jobs at various levels in different industries – from 'sweeping up in the local factory to senior partner in Price Waterhouse' as one sponsor put it; school-leavers specifically skilled for a technological work environment; and school-leavers inculcated with entrepreneurial and individualistic attitudes in keeping with a society freed from socialism, bureaucracy and dependency.

Not all the motivation for sponsorship derived from a direct concern with the nature of the labour force or with the need for a more technologically oriented curriculum. For example, in seeking to transform its voluntary controlled boys' and girls' schools in New Cross (south-east London) into a CTC, the Haberdashers' Company was also concerned to protect the schools' sixth forms and academic ethos from possible threat by an ambivalent LEA. Funds were also needed for updating buildings and facilities which neither the ILEA nor its successor authority, Lewisham, was in a position to provide. The CTC option was pursued in preference to grant-maintained status partly because it was first on the scene, but also because it appeared that more funds would be attached to that route to independence. The Southwark Diocesan Board of Education of the Church of England was motivated by similar considerations in relocating to Docklands a voluntary aided school in urgent need of new accommodation. Despite its dilapidated and dispersed buildings, the DES had twice refused to approve the necessary capital expenditure for Bacon's to move to the Surrey Docks as a maintained comprehensive school. Changing its status to a CTC brought the necessary change of mind.

Both the move and the new status were described by the

diocesan education director as offering an exceptional opportunity to enhance the school's Christian ethos. In Gateshead, the opportunity to create such a school seems to have been the main impetus behind what was, despite Baroness Cox's involvement, very much a local initiative. Emmanuel's lead sponsor, Peter Vardy, became involved after a personal approach from a group of Tyneside evangelical Christians who recognised how the CTC route could be used to establish a new, mostly state-funded but independent Christian school. His fellow sponsors and local businessmen David Vardy and Albert Dicken belonged to the same evangelical church. To David Vardy, it was an opportunity to make Christian belief

> an integral part of the ethos of the college, not in any doctrinaire sense, but that the lifestyle of the staff and the whole character of the college should represent the sort of moral standards that were valued years ago but now seem to have been sadly lost, and to ensure that within the students there is respect for authority, they see the family unit as important, there is respect for parents, concern for other members of society.

To reinforce that view, one of Emmanuel's main corporate sponsors was described by a representative as having been strongly attracted by the prospect of 'a CTC set up on basic Christian principles and traditions . . . where family values and Christian standards . . . were presented and would be underpinning the whole education process'.

It was argued in the opening chapters that the origins of CTCs lie in a variety of policy sets. This has become even more marked during the initiative's implementation, especially in the coexistence of attempts to 'modernise' the workforce and break away from a 'dependency culture' with a reassertion of traditional Christian values. Some apparently incongruous modes of discourse within CTC publicity, illustrated by the strategic objective defined in Bacon's 1991 prospectus as 'to promote values appropriate to the Christian ethos of the College within the framework of total quality management', are particular examples of what Ball (1990) characterises as a struggle within the CTC movement between the 'discourse of vocational progressivism' and that of the 'cultural restorationists'. As the initiative has progressed, it is possible to discern shifts in the rhetoric of legitimation between the theme of modernisation and those two key components of Thatcherism, the neo-liberal commitment to market forces and the neo-conservative attachment to traditional values. CTCs thus embody many of the tensions in what Dale (1989) terms the Thatcherite policy of 'conservative modernisation', and we explore these tensions further in chapter 7.

Links with the past, and with traditional forms of educational provision, are also symbolised by the involvement of the City livery companies. Although this is sometimes seen as a deviation from the original conception of business sponsorship, they were clearly eligible under the terms of the initial prospectus for CTCs, which spoke of 'business, industrial and charitable promoters' (DES 1986). The Haberdashers' Company's interest in converting its voluntary controlled schools into a CTC was partly influenced by its experience of running independent schools elsewhere, although it was unusual in being the only sponsor of the CTC in Hatcham and because its only significant contribution was the buildings used by its existing schools. The Mercers' Company, benefactors of the St Paul's Schools in London and with a long history of supporting private education, showed an early interest in making a more direct investment in the initiative. Although its first attempt to sponsor a CTC in Bexley was thwarted, it became the lead sponsor for the CTC established on a greenfield site in Telford New Town, Shropshire. Although it proved abortive, the attempt to enlist the support of the Merchant Venturers Society for a CTC in Bristol was another potential continuity with educational charities of the past since the society's nineteenth-century college in Bristol laid the foundation for the engineering schools of Bristol and Bath Universities and for Bristol Polytechnic (now the University of the West of England at Bristol).

The incorporation into the CTC programme of a long-standing proposal for a performing arts school indicates the considerable elasticity of the original concept. It also demonstrates the willingness of the government to respond to the particular predilections of potential sponsors in order to keep the initiative going. It was because Baker's plan to establish a pilot programme of twenty CTCs by 1990 was already in some difficulties that the wording of Section 105 of the Education Reform Act 1988 not only gave the CTCs a statutory basis and their sponsors some security, but also created the entirely new concept of a City College for the Technology of the Arts (CCTA). A curriculum emphasis on 'technology in its application to the performing and creative arts' satisfied the particular interests of Richard Branson, founder of Virgin Records, and the British Recording Industry Trust, and led to the creation of a special CTC in Croydon which also departed from the initial model by providing for a 13/14–18 age range and having a largely undefined catchment area. Given the public images of some of the other sponsors, there is no doubt that involving Richard Branson was a public relations coup. Yet the ensuing press coverage, often concentrating on a somewhat misleading analogy with New York's La Guardia High School (and its television embodiment in the series *Fame*) only added confusion to public perceptions of what the programme was actually about – as did the eventual decision to call the CCTA the Performing Arts and Technology School.

We have concentrated more on the motives of sponsors than on the methods of finding them. That task, and what proved to be an even greater problem of finding appropriate sites, was clearly beyond the capacity of the small CTC unit within the DES even if the search had been an appropriate use of civil servants' time. Responsibility for finding both sponsors and sites was therefore given early in 1987 to Cyril Taylor, an old friend of Kenneth Baker's. Taylor had been an executive in the USA for the 'Gleam' toothpaste company, and had made his fortune running education programmes for overseas students and transforming a neo-Gothic training college for Methodist ministers in Richmond into the first US-style college in England. As we noted earlier, his own proposal for a network of technical schools outside of LEA control had been one of the influences on the development of the CTC policy and he had argued then that such schools should be concentrated in inner city areas (Taylor 1986: 30). Taylor worked initially from within the DES, but in May 1987, he was appointed chairman of the City Technology College Trust, created ostensibly to place an independent body between the government and its new category of state-independent schools. With a council membership characterised not unfairly as being composed of 'the rich and the Right' (*The Teacher* 8 June 1987), its political character seemed more apparent than its independence and Taylor himself (subsequently knighted for his efforts) had been deputy

Conservative leader on the GLC and was a director of the Centre for Policy Studies. In the following year, Susan Fey was made the Trust's chief executive and immediately strengthened its co-ordinating function. Baker's first choice for the post had been Chris Webb, who had worked with him on creating IT centres when Baker was at the Department of Trade and Industry and who subsequently became chief education officer for Islington. But Susan Fey's appointment was a shrewd one. Though married to a Conservative MP, she had considerable credibility as an experienced educator and current principal of Morley Adult Education College in Southwark. Describing her appointment as a 'triumph' for the Secretary of State, the *Times Educational Supplement* emphasised in her profile a long commitment to improving inner-city education and a particular interest in doing so through curriculum innovation (10 September 1988). We describe in later chapters the Trust's role in implementing the 'curriculum mission' of CTCs, and are concerned here with its own entrepreneurial activities. At the local level, these were entrusted from early in 1988 to project directors who would oversee the creation of a CTC from the first sounding out of sponsors through the negotiation of a site to the construction and opening of the building.

THE SECURING OF SITES

As the concept of a CTC had to be adjusted to attract sponsors, so had the definition of where CTCs should be. Of the eight specific locations listed by the DES in 1986, all already part of inner-city initiatives, only 'north-central' Middlesbrough has a CTC. Of the eighteen other urban areas identified as 'possible', those which continued to prove impossible have included Liverpool, Manchester, Southampton and Hull (see Table 3.1). Of the successful projects, neither Corby nor Telford fits the initial inner-city image and Telford emerged only after unsuccessful searches in Portsmouth and Walsall. There were also unsuccessful projects in Lincoln and Barnet, which seem even less likely locations. The heavy concentration of CTCs in souph-east London is also as much at variance with the original blueprint for a national network as are the large gaps in the industrial north.

Yet it was the nature of the initiative that its implementation was considerably shaped by chance and persuasion. David Regan's comment that the DES 'never imposed a CTC unbidden on any town' (1990: 23) is curious, given that it could impose nothing without 'substantial contributions' of private money. The accompanying comment that each CTC 'is essentially the product of local initiative' is also a dubious generalisation, given the 'arm-twisting' of potential sponsors described earlier. A DES official suggested to us that the task of finding sites might have been eased if the government had used compulsory purchase powers instead of moving by persuasion. It seems more likely that the use of such powers would have deterred some sponsors by intensifying already fierce local opposition. As it was, the likelihood of opposition led to considerable secrecy in the initial negotiations and to predictable complaints about lack of consultation. One project director described vividly to us the difficulties of negotiating for a site when the DES controlled the purse-strings and its officials insisted that he told the LEAs and schools affected nothing until the Secretary of State was prepared to confirm the proposal. By that time, the announcement 'came as a bombshell'. Although admitting the high risk of 'an immediate backlash from local interest groups at the mere sniff of a CTC', the Trust's director for development claimed that he made 'a special point of discussing our proposals with LEAs in our project areas so as to get cooperation over sites and over drawing catchment so as to minimise impact on existing schools' (*Times Educational Supplement* 14 October 1988). The claim was emphatically denied in our interviews with chief education officers in five CTC locations. In one of them, formal notification of the project came three months after its extensive reporting in the local press.

From Susan Fey's educationist perspective, the ideal was 'what we laughingly call in polluted areas a greenfield site ... a completely empty site so you build a school which is built for a curriculum and around a curriculum'. From a Treasury perspective, a redundant school already closed was ideal because renovation rather than rebuilding might be sufficient. Even if the school had to be pulled down, its site was likely to be relatively cheap because its future use was restricted to educational purposes and could not just be sold (for example) for housing. The progress of the initiative therefore depended above all on LEAs' willingness to make such sites available. It seems that ministers took false comfort from the rapid evaporation of immediate LEA opposition to TVEI. That analogy was inappropriate. TVEI promised enough new money to maintained schools to offset objections to its source and to the strings attached. The CTC initiative, however, was explicitly targeted at the very LEAs most likely to have their reorganisation plans disrupted and to contain schools of the kind which CTCs were intended to challenge or even replace. It is true that several Labour-controlled LEAs initially chose not to reject the CTC initiative out of hand, but rather to explore its elasticity to the limits. Thus both Manchester and Avon made proposals during 1986 and 1987 for using the programme to fund new technology initiatives within maintained schools. Another Labour LEA even considered putting itself forward as a sponsor. Even though later proposals for voluntary-aided CTCs, and the subsequent Technology Schools Initiative, suggest that these ideas were far from outlandish, they were rejected by government at the time as inconsistent with the political aims of the programme, thereby adding weight to the view that independence from LEA control was indeed its key component.

The most obvious reason for LEA opposition was the anticipated effects of a CTC on other secondary schools in its catchment area. All the directors of education that we interviewed, except Donald Naismith, who had actively encouraged the establishment of CTCs in both Croydon and Wandsworth, pointed to the irony of being faced with the establishment of new schools in the very areas in which they were being asked by the government and by the Audit Commission to phase out surplus places. As Susan Fey herself pointed out, a few urban areas (like Tower Hamlets) needed new schools; it could also be argued that the predicted rise in school rolls from the mid-1990s made a case for new provision in inner-city areas as part of their regeneration and as an encouragement to people not to move out. But in the short run, CTCs seemed to 'come in like an unguided missile and make their lives incredibly difficult'.

Difficulty was unavoidable, given the intended location of CTCs where 'the education system is at present most under pressure' (DES 1986: 2). From an LEA perspective, the rationalisation of provision was part of that pressure because these were the areas where secondary rolls were likely to be falling most sharply. Donald Naismith was unusual in seeing the sale of a 'failing' secondary school to the CTC Trust as beneficial to LEA planning, though Kent's sale of the Downs School in Dartford is also partly explained in this way. Croydon had 'suffered one of the sharpest demographic downturns in the whole country', losing 'about 43 per cent of our secondary population in the 1980s' and so having to close a number of schools. When it came to Naismith's notice that 'sites were being sought for CTCs ... it struck me that it might provide some answers to some of the problems at Sylvan school'. Other chief education officers (CEOs) saw the consequences as Maureen O'Connor (1986) had done when the programme was first announced – namely that 'one pupil's CTC is another pupil's school closure'. Newcastle's director of education deplored the pressure on business and industry to 'invest money in superfluous and unwanted schools in an area already facing very serious problems of falling rolls, declining resources and excess places' (*The Journal* 15 July 1988). The 'unwanted' school of which he was complaining would have its main effect on Gateshead, which then estimated its over-capacity in secondary provision at 40 per cent. In another LEA which had closed nine secondary schools since 1981, taking out in the process more than five thousand places, its CEO commented to us:

> Now it's not a lot of fun persuading people that their school has got to be closed. There must be a way of going to a meeting and saying – I'm your local friend the CEO and I've come to close your school'. There must be a way in which that gets a standing ovation, like Baker at the party conference, but in my experience all it gets is a blank stare and a room filled with blood, mostly mine.

If the risk of that dismal experience was much higher in urban areas, the Association of Metropolitan Authorities (1987) giving it prominence among its many objections to CTCs, it was also true that most of the 'possible locations' indicated by the DES (1986) were in the territory of Labour-controlled councils. It is not surprising, then, that the disadvantages of housing a CTC were more likely to be confronted and their advantages emphasised where the Conservatives were in control. Solihull sold a redundant school. Bradford changed tack when the Conservatives took over in 1988, thereby allowing Stanley Kalms to complete, in a city where his company (Dixon's) had a particularly strong presence, a sponsorship deal he had been pursuing unsuccessfully in several other northern cities. Conservative-controlled Kent, Croydon and Wandsworth offered positive cooperation. At Middlesbrough and Gateshead, council resistance could be circumvented because the Catholic diocesan authority (to the displeasure of the LEA in each case) was willing to spend on its other schools the capital proceeds of selling a school site it no longer needed. This was a form of 'compensation' which Cyril Taylor accused LEAs of denying themselves through a politically inspired intransigence which he compared with resistance to the sale of council houses (*Times Educational Supplement* 28 October 1988). Elsewhere, however, it was the Church authorities which were blamed for impeding progress. This was notably the case in Liverpool, where Stuart Sexton accused both the Catholic Archbishop Warlock and the Anglican Bishop Shepherd of 'political' resistance to selling appropriate sites. In Bradford and Corby, sites were made available by sponsors themselves, while Hanson recouped some of its expenditure at Solihull by selling land to the Nottingham CTC. Another way of circumventing objections, and also of associating the CTC initiative more generally with urban policy, was to seek sites in urban development areas where planning permission from the local authority was not required. Although this was done successfully in the London Docklands, where the London Docklands Development Corporation (LDDC) helped to sponsor community facilities for Bacon's College, prospective urban development sites in Machester and Bristol failed to materialise.

With all these difficulties, it is not surprising that the actual siting of CTCs differs considerably from the DES map of 1986, though their distance from the originally targeted locations can be exaggerated. Some catchment areas were drawn so as to extend into Labour-controlled and 'inner-city' areas. Thus Kingshurst draws pupils from Birmingham as well as Solihull, and Harris CTC recruits from Lambeth, Southwark and Lewisham as well as Croydon. As we show in chapter 4, it is difficult for critics to sustain the argument that CTCs have been situated in socially advantaged areas and so lost what had been a main rhetorical justification. What was certainly a controversial outcome of the difficulties we have described was a tactical reinterpretation of the initial promise to create twenty 'new' schools.

'We are approaching councils like Croydon, Bexley and Kent and asking them to sell us the most deprived or failing school', wrote Cyril Taylor (*Times Educational Supplement* 17 June 1988). 'Instead of creating a new school which threatens others, we will try to make the existing school better.'

Since a newly built school would be especially costly in the south-east, it is unsurprising that the CTCs which incorporate existing schools – Harris, Leigh, Bacon's and Haberdashers'- are in the London area. But for the tactic to work at all, the definition of a 'failing' school has had to be very flexible indeed. There has also had to be considerable adjustment to the government's professed belief in parental choice.

The Downs school in Dartford was the nearest to Taylor's notion of transforming an existing school. By 1988 it was seriously under-subscribed and identified for closure or for being changed into something else in every LEA reorganisation document. A senior LEA official described it to us as split site, poorly led, losing pupils so fast that its 'wide ability' label was a euphemism for secondary modern, 'in serious decline', and requiring drastic action. When the LEA was approached by the CTC Trust as a consequence of Taylor's strategy, it saw an opportunity to get rid of a school which was not worth keeping in its present form but which it could not afford to revive from its own resources. As a member of staff in the successor Leigh CTC told us, 'Kent wanted to get rid of the Downs, it was a nuisance . . . and for somebody else to come along and say they'd take it was almost too good to be true'. It was also encouraged in that view by Bob Dunn, whose constituency Dartford was.

For another Conservative-controlled council, however, an apparently similar project went badly wrong. A proposal to transform the Riverside school in Bexley was the fifth notional CTC to be announced in December 1987. That it failed was attributed by the Trust to the Thamesmead Development Corporation's asking too much for the site, and by the leader of a well-organised local campaign to an affirmation of 'the right of parents to keep their neighbourhood school, which is successful and thriving'. Although the school's intake of 125 in 1987 was well below its standard number of 167, it was very much a neighbourhood school, was the first choice of a large and rising number of parents, had a reasonable academic record and a low unemployment rate among its leavers in an area where youth unemployment generally was high. Its staff flatly denied that it was either 'deprived or failing', and 90 per cent of parents in a 62 per cent ballot were against the CTC proposal. Jack Straw commented that 'if this were a GMS [grant-maintained school] proposal, it would now fail' (*Times Educational Supplement* 16 September 1988). The government's own arguments were energetically turned against it by the leader of the parents' campaign. As she told us:

> At that time, Kenneth Baker was saying 'parental power, parental choice' and we really threw that right back at him and said, 'Right, you are telling us we have a choice and this is our choice. We don't want what you're offering us.' And there was a Hansard come out, and Kenneth Baker said, 'There is no reason to close a [good] school to re-open it as a CTC'. And we really played on that as well because Riverside *is* a good school. ... And when you know that if your kids don't get into Riverside they're going to have to be bused all over Thamesmead, it's just not on ... you'd get kids coming from all over – almost up to Dartford the catchment area went – and our kids going further away.

At Sylvan school in Croydon, however, a similarly strong parental campaign was ignored rather than defeated. As noted earlier, the director of education viewed it as a failing school or at least as sufficiently unpopular with Croydon parents to justify the LEA in disposing of it. The disposal took place over the heads of governors and staff, the proposal appearing in the local press before they had been notified and being timed for the end of the summer term (so the chair and vice-chair of governors claimed) to impede prompt organisation of opposition. Although the school was under-subscribed, its intake from adjacent boroughs was rising. Far from 'failing' academically, it had recently been cited by the LEA for good practice in several curriculum areas and commended by Kenneth Baker (after a visit) for its preparations for GCSE. The 97 per cent parental 'no' to the CTC proposal, in a ballot organised by the local council of churches after consulting the Electoral Reform Society, was declared invalid by the authority even though it represented an absolute majority of the parents entitled to vote, and ignored by the Secretary of State when he approved the proposal in May 1989. Again, the contrast with the government's attitude to opting out is sharp. In the context of recent government references to 'restoring the balance' in grant-maintained (GM) ballots by restricting LEAs' use of 'considerably greater resources to try to undermine governing bodies' attempts to inform parents properly about the GM option' (DFE 1992: para 7.6), we should also note a strong feeling among the defenders of Sylvan whom we interviewed that the CTC proposal had been promoted with far greater resources and much glossier, more extensive publicity than they could match.

While charges of education failure were made and refuted at Riverside and Sylvan, they could not be made at all about the two Haberdashers' schools. They had been consistently in the ILEA's top category through its annual comparisons 1986–9 of actual examination performance with what could reasonably be 'expected' of each of its secondary schools, given their intakes and circumstances. They were also, however, voluntary schools, so that as with Bacon's CTC the change could be made against strong LEA objections. It went ahead despite considerable well-publicised opposition by Parents Against a Technology College for Hatcham (PATCH) and a negative vote by the parents from the girls' school. Like the other campaigns referred to, there were many objections from parents that their own choice of school was effectively being taken away.

THE FUNDING OF CTCs

If finding sponsors and sites in the 'right' areas was difficult enough, securing sponsorship at the level which the government had hoped for proved impossible. The target was certainly set rashly high. As defined by the DES (1986: 8), 'the principle of funding will be that the promoters will meet all or a substantial part of the capital costs'. The only reasonable interpretation of that statement is that business and industry were to be the major shareholders in the venture. Yet by the time of the first full Commons debate on the initiative, during which Kenneth Baker insisted that no educational venture this century had attracted such support from the private sector, the £30 million or so private money which had been given or pledged was outmatched by some £93 million public money already committed to the programme. The disparity prompted Jack Straw to complain that 'the government's original intention of setting up public schools with private money has now changed to setting up private schools with public money' (quoted in *Education* 8 July 1988).

The vulnerability of the programme to such charges was heightened by repeated claims that little of the money pledged from private sources had actually been paid, and that ministerial references to the extent of private funding deliberately overstated it by running the cash and the promises together. The large gaps between them were indicated by the minister in response to a Commons question (Table 3.3), and were large enough to raise further questions both about the auditing of the programme and about whether sponsors' full involvement in the affairs of 'their' CTC should await full payment of the contributions which had been promised.

Table 3.3 Sponsorship money promised and received

	Promised (£ million)	Received (£ million)
Kinghurst	1.982	1.450
Djanogly	1.882	1.040
Macmillan	1.485	1.450
Emmanuel	1.600	0.238
Bradford	2.265	1.526
Harris	1.500	0.300
Performing Arts	4.100	0.594
Bacon's	2.500	0.000
Derby	1.150	0.234
Telford	2.000	0.000
Corby	1.660	0.000

Source: Figures taken from a Commons reply by Angela Rumbold, the Schools Minister, 6 July 1990

It was soon clear that even if all promises were fulfilled, the private stake in the CTC programme would amount to no more than 20 per cent of capital expenditure, a proportion strikingly at variance with the government's initial statement of 'the principle of funding'. This misjudgement has led to an unforeseen commitment of well over £100 million public money to keep the programme going, and made the government by far the major shareholder in the enterprise. Such misjudgement has sometimes been attributed to underestimating the costs of building new secondary schools, but this is unlikely. When the director of the Industrial Society complained that 'the

Department of Education must be living in a fantasy world if it thinks companies can afford to spend five or six million pounds on one particular project', he had in mind a 'substantial' contribution but not an especially expensive school.[3] Indeed, DES control over the total cost was both tight and detailed. Speaking in 1991, by which time sponsorship had settled down to the minor share, a project director explained the nature of that control:

> So you have £10 million of which £2 million must be found by the sponsors and £8 million will be found by the DES. Then you think that . . . you're going to be free to build the school for these kinds of costs, disposing as you wish, and then you find that they've tied it down in terms of the cost of the site, the amount of money to be spent on the building, the amount of money on furniture and equipment, and so you find various heads of expenditure emerging supposedly as guidelines but becoming quite definitive.

While not miscalculating the cost of new schools, the DES underestimated the strength and persistence of LEA opposition to releasing the sites of those which were empty or otherwise redundant. The effect has been a much higher proportion of new building than was anticipated in 1986. Trust representatives insisted to us that refurbishing a run-down building was not much less expensive than building a new one, which may have been true of the 'failing' schools which were supposedly the target of transformation. Even then, a main sponsor described vividly his successful attempt to persuade the DES that it was a new building altogether which was needed:

> We went to London and they said, 'You're in charge, you're in control, you do whatever you like'. So I said, 'Well, that's marvellous'. 'But there's a school at —— and we've got the plans here'. And it was an old clasp building, shocking things, built in the 1960s in a rush. 'And we would like you to have a look at that'. So I took the pictures away and I said, 'I don't want this . . . we're not doing up the old school, we're knocking the school down and building a new one . . . if we tart the thing up it will last another ten years and there'll be a fortune to spend again. So I said, 'I want to build something that we're all proud of, that stands there like a beacon on the

hill . . . when I came down here you said I had a clean sheet of paper and I could start again. 'Ah but, but, you know.' And I said, 'No buts, either I knock the school down, I build a new school, or I'm not interested'. 'Ay alright, you can knock the school down'. So I got myself a new school. . . . It will be the best one in the country.

DES officials may well have been unpractised in negotiations of that kind.

The mounting cost of the CTC programme and of the government's stake in it brought predictable criticism of using public money to create 'independent' schools when the state of maintained school buildings (especially secondary schools) has been a matter of increasing concern.[4] It has been argued by the programme's political promoters that its cost was being met from 'new' money, and that spread around it would have amounted to about £1,800 per school and achieved nothing. But the coincidence of the programme with substantial cuts in capital expenditure in the maintained system, and with repeated HMI warnings about the increasingly dilapidated state of school buildings, has prompted hostile comparisons. 'Just what sort of public education initiative is it', asked a *TES* editorial, 'which puts up £9 million from public funds for a private school? And just what sort of priorities are being pursued when one, as yet unbuilt, private school gets £9.05 million while the county of Nottinghamshire's entire capital allocation is less than £2.5 million?' (27 March 1988). Though the figures varied, the Nottingham comparison was made frequently – for example, by the NUT (1989: 3–4). Jack Straw compared government capital spending of £27 million on CTCs in Bradford, Gateshead, Croydon and Dartford with the £28 million capital allocation for 1,218 other schools in those LEAs – figures which he then interpreted literally as a contrast between £6,484 and £78 per pupil (cited in *Guardian* 17 November 1990). The chief education officer for one of those LEAs commented to us that the £7 million which the government was paying towards the CTC in his area 'is, on the going rate, about seven years of capital allocation from the DES to this authority for the entire capital programme' (interview, 1 November 1990). Another critic noted that the government was then spending more on a few CTCs than it was on introducing the National Curriculum in 30,000 schools (Chitty 1989: 4).

The recurrent funding of CTCs has also been contentious. In the 1986 DES prospectus, it was defined as being 'at a level of assistance per pupil comparable with what is provided by LEAs for maintained schools serving similar catchment areas'. The subsequent revenue report commissioned by the CTC Trust illustrates that lack of planning to which we referred at the beginning of the chapter. For CTC catchment areas normally cover parts of several LEAs, of which one or more may have substantial suburban and 'county' districts within them. The appropriate per capita grant is therefore redefined, in a late draft of the frequently redrafted funding agreement, as being 'based on units of calculation ... derived from averages of expenditure by LEAs on secondary schools located in urban areas similar to those in which the CTCs are located'. Even then, the government's funding formula is regarded within the CTC movement as underestimating the extent of social deprivation in the kinds of inner-city area from which most of their intake is supposed to be drawn. It is also seen as seriously under-estimating the start-up costs of new schools, the running and depreciation costs of unusually extensive IT facilities, and the additional staff and premises costs created by a markedly longer teaching day and school year.[5] In the Trust's view, schools seen as being funded in luxury by their critics are perceived from within as being underfunded for the demanding 'mission' they have been set.

In this chapter, we have described how the original CTC blueprint has been changed in critical respects. The balance between public and private funding has been greatly altered, the definition of appropriate locations has been modified, the science and technology orientation has been broadened and somewhat weakened, and the notion of a network of 'new' schools imaginatively interpreted. The difficulties we have outlined have contributed to doubts about the strength of government support for the programme, especially after the departure from the DES of the Secretary of State whose personal initiative it is often seen to be. Certainly his successors have sometimes seemed lukewarm, each denying at times any intention of expanding the programme in its original, highly expensive form. We examine in chapter 6 the growing emphasis on the cheaper option of developing voluntary-aided and grant-maintained CTCs, a strategy which Sir Cyril Taylor has promoted energetically, and place that approach in the wider context of policies designed to produce more diversified and specialised forms of secondary education. It is commonplace that policy initiatives designed to serve certain objectives are often considerably reshaped by those charged with implementing them. In this chapter, we have drawn particular attention to the reshaping necessary because the CTC initiative was badly planned and certainly underplanned. Chapter 4 explores in detail the kinds of pupils for whom CTCs were intended, and the kinds of intake they have recruited. We then take up in chapter 5 the reshaping of the initiative within the CTCs themselves by those, charged with implementing it, whose purposes and priorities have sometimes been rather different from what its political architects had primarily in mind.

Choosers and chosen

The 'fresh opportunities' which CTCs are intended to provide place them in a long tradition of constructing educational escape routes for deserving individuals from the 'limitations' of their social background and of the schooling otherwise available. But this particular educational 'ladder' differs significantly from what had been constructed before. The traditional assumption has been that equality of opportunity means access on merit, unimpeded by capacity to pay, to grammar schools and their equivalent in the private sector. It was typical of this view that among the 'basic truths' proclaimed in the fourth *Black Papers* was the assertion that a vain pursuit of equality had seriously disadvantaged 'the clever working-class child in a deprived area' who 'stands little chance of a real academic education' without some form of selection (Cox and Boyson 1975: 2). The Assisted Places Scheme reasserted that belief by opening independent schools of entirely traditional academic 'excellence' to 'able children from less well-off homes' who can meet those schools' normal selection criteria. One of its principal ministerial promoters has commented on the illogicality from a market perspective of limiting this extension of parental choice to parents fortunate enough to have 'able' children.[1] But given the success of the private sector in asserting a causal connection between independence and 'academic excellence', it is unsurprising that the schools themselves have treated assisted places as academic scholarships.

To hostile observers, the CTCs represented an addition to this elite segment of the education system. They were therefore predicted to become 'subsidised grammar schools in high technology clothes', initiating a return to academic selection and the social divisiveness associated with it (Glazier 1986; Benn

1987; Chitty 1987). Drawing very different conclusions from a similarly hierarchical perspective, others welcomed the 'new choice of school' as a potentially high-status alternative to traditionally academic secondary education. As Stanley Kalms, lead sponsor of Dixon's CTC, put it: 'We are looking for problem solvers rather than academics, the kind of kids who like taking their toys apart, kids who play with computers' (quoted in *Yorkshire Post* 27 February 1989). If such defenders of CTCs had been inclined to cite research evidence in their support, they might have drawn on that 'political arithmetic' strand in the sociology of education which documented the relative success of technically oriented selective secondary education in attracting pupils from a wider range of social backgrounds than the grammar schools had done (Halsey *et al.* 1980: 148–73; Heath 1980). For that is how CTCs have primarily been presented, by their political sponsors and from within the 'movement'. They are to be not only fully comprehensive in their intakes, but to provide special opportunities for children who might otherwise be left adrift. As the lead sponsor of another CTC argued:

> If they're clever and come from advantaged backgrounds, they don't need this school as much as the others. We are setting out to help the kids from these areas. If we don't achieve that, we're wasting our time, I've wasted my money, because the clever kids from the good backgrounds would probably do well anyway.

In this chapter, we first examine the constraints which the government placed on CTCs to secure intakes 'representative of the community they serve'. We then explore how the CTCs have managed the selection of suitable children when the demand for places has considerably exceeded the supply, and when critics have been alert to any sign of their becoming subsidised technological grammar schools. In the second half of the chapter, we consider in more detail the kinds of children and parents who have chosen and been chosen by two particular CTCs.

INTAKES 'REPRESENTATIVE OF THE COMMUNITY THEY SERVE'

As defined in their initial remit, CTCs were to 'serve a substantial catchment area' and would not normally take children from outside it. They would be required, 'as a condition of grant', to admit pupils 'spanning the full range of ability' found in that catchment area who would also be 'representative' of its social and ethnic composition. But CTCs could not be 'neighbourhood schools taking all comers', because their pupils had to be demonstrably willing and able to benefit from the special character of the education they offered. Brief guidance was then offered about the criteria which CTCs should use to select their entrants – criteria which included their own 'general aptitude' and 'readiness to take advantage of' a distinctive kind of education, and also their parents' commitment to 'full-time education or training up to the age of 18' and to the CTC's curriculum and ethos (DES 1986: 5).

These criteria are retained in the funding agreements which each CTC signs with the government, and the constraints they impose are unusual. At a time when the government has introduced 'open enrolment' to maintained schools, subject only to their physical capacity, and has enhanced parents' right to choose secondary schools outside the LEA in which they live, CTCs are unusual in having clear catchment areas. The consequent difficulties are illustrated in this extract from a project director's report to his CTC's governing body on admissions for September 1991.

> In both —— and ——, some problems of catchment demarcation arose. For the most part, these doubts were resolved by accepting the authority to which the community charge was paid as the area of residence. The largest residence problem surrounded those parents who indicated that they were about to move. or would move into the area if they were offered a place. The panel decided that in such cases the parent must produce firm evidence of a commitment to residence by January 31, in the form of a contract to purchase or to rent within the area. Since there was no guarantee that other parents had not falsified their addresses, they too were asked to provide evidence of residence.

Unlike other CTCs, the Performing Arts and Technology School is permitted to recruit at 14 from the whole of Greater London because of its uniquely specialised character, and from what is effectively a national catchment area at 16. ADT recruits from ten London boroughs, though 50 per cent of its places are reserved for Wandsworth; the boundaries around several other CTC catchment areas have been altered since their original mapping to secure a more balanced intake; and there has been a general widening of the area on which a CTC can draw.[2] But these are adjustments to a strategy which Sir Cyril Taylor described at interview as a thoroughly illogical departure from the government's commitment to parental choice.

> The Act unfortunately defines the catchment area for a CTC. I've tried to increase that each year. The civil servants wanted tight lines, but 5,000 [children of secondary school age] was ludicrous, it would mean that another school would have to close. Now we're getting it up to 15,000–20,000. You know, a catchment area should basically be whatever is within reasonable travelling distance, probably a maximum of forty-five minutes each way. . . . I said at the time, 'This is nonsense, why should CTCs have a catchment area when maintained schools don't?'

The most obvious explanaton for designating the area which CTCs should serve is the explanation which Sir Cyril Taylor dismissed as being inadequate even on its own terms – namely to limit effects on recruitment to other schools by dispersing their intakes. Given the location of most CTCs in urban areas where secondary school rolls have fallen especially sharply, this might seem a sensible attempt to construct a defence similar to that made against criticisms that the Assisted Places Scheme would 'cream off' able, well-motivated pupils. Indeed, the Association for Science Education (1986: 3) saw a 'striking similarity' between the catchment area of a CTC and 'the domain from which a typical grammar school population was drawn'. It therefore warned against another 'siphoning off the ablest and best-motivated from the locality . . . thus adversely affecting the quality of the provision for the majority'. But while thirty assisted places a year was a typical allocation to the former direct-grant grammar schools and other independent day schools which dominate the Assisted Places Scheme, a CTC recruiting 150–80 pupils a year presented obvious dangers to some neighbouring schools.

CTC catchment areas have been drawn with care. We doubt whether avoiding unnecessary damage to particular maintained schools was a significant factor in that exercise, despite the claim cited in chapter 3, because consultation with the LEAs affected has been rare. The main consideration is to uphold the image of new inner-city (or at least urban) secondary schools enabled by their freedom from LEA control to show what can be achieved in areas more usually associated with low staying-on rates and educational failure. Despite the immediate protests against 'backdoor' selection, it is politically necessary that CTCs should be seen to succeed with intakes 'representative' of areas with high levels of social disadvantage. Representativeness of 'the community they serve' is, however, a difficult concept by normal definitions of 'community', because catchment areas of the size attached to CTCs are unlikely to have any common identity. Indeed, those areas seem to be – and are intended to be – collections of districts of very different social character. This can be illustrated by Solihull, which evoked caustic comment when announced as the site for the first CTC because it seemed so unlike the more obviously 'deprived' west Midlands locations of Handsworth, Sandwell and Wolverhampton which the DES had listed as possibilities in 1986. But Solihull had been created as a borough in 1974 from three sharply contrasting areas. Kingshurst is sited in the north of the borough, where most housing is on council overspill estates originating from Birmingham's slum clearances of the 1960s, and is within a mile of the predominantly working-class area of east Birmingham. When the initial catchment area appeared to be too down-market, the middle-class districts of Castle Bromwich and Sheldon were added in 1989 (Walford and Miller 1991: 20–6, 105–7). Djanogly's catchment was defined to give it both a relatively local character, and (initially) to exclude the nearby but inappropriately affluent district of Mapperley Park. Emmanuel's catchment area includes several 'problem areas' in Newcastle, and excludes relatively prosperous districts in the west of Gateshead. In so far as these and similar social mapping exercises initially created appropriately disadvantaged catchment areas for the 'exceptional' opportunities which CTCs are claimed to offer, then they carry an obvious risk to the high level of academic performance which they will also be expected to achieve. For if the ability range of their intakes is to 'represent' the catchment area rather than the national distribution of test scores, then it is likely to be downwardly skewed. We return to this aspect of representativeness later in the chapter.

In these social engineering respects, the DES requirements may have been paved with good (or at least politic) intentions, but they are also impractical. This was the main conclusion of an independent study, financed by the DES but then denied funding for the further, longitudinal investigation which the research team recommended. Professor Roger Murphy and his colleagues from Nottingham University were asked to establish whether a sample of CTCs were meeting 'the admission criteria set out by the Department', and whether their selection process 'is fair, efficient and economical'. The commission reflected DES alarm at the escalating difficulties and cost of CTC selection procedures as the number of applications rose, but the team were unprepared for the hostility which their findings aroused among the CTCs themselves. Interviewed by us long after the fuss had died down, Susan Fey was still indignant at what she regarded as the researchers' political naivety in not realising how their findings would be taken out of context by the CTCs' many persistent critics. Their lack of care in 'finding the right words', she argued, had undone a great deal of hard statistical work to establish that 'what we were doing was very, very fair, in line with equal opportunities, open and above board'. Given the widespread belief that CTCs were enabled to be academically selective because of their unusual capacity to choose the pupils they took in, the sensitivity is understandable. Yet the CTC reaction to the report seems a case both of blaming the messenger, and of expecting researchers to modify their findings through anticipating public response. In fact, the report's main conclusion was not to blame the four CTCs whose selection procedures had been studied, but rather to reject the task they had been set. 'The criteria as laid down by the DES are collectively unworkable, and no College could have hoped to have satisfied such criteria as they are currently specified' (Murphy *et al.* 1990: 10). The account of the report in the *Times Educational Supplement* (a journal perceived within the CTC movement as consistently hostile) was accurately headlined 'CTC selectors face an "impossible task".' But the gist of the item itself was to highlight the lack of evidence that CTC intakes reflected the full ability range, or that 'a true racial and social mix has been achieved' (21 September 1990). The research team's justification for their main conclusion provides a useful introduction to our own account of how CTCs have approached the task of selecting their pupils.

First, the representativeness of intakes, socially and in their range of ability, required detailed baseline data from the relevant catchment area which are not already available and which CTCs cannot be expected to collect for themselves. Second, the fitness of applicants (and their parents) to benefit from a 'distinctive' form of secondary education, and their commitment to it, had to be assessed before any distinctive characteristics had been established, publicised and realistically compared with what was available in conventional schools. Third, judgements had to be made about the suitability of individual applicants in relation to specified criteria while at the same time keeping in mind the accompanying requirements about the intake as a whole. Thus although Susan Fey complained that the report had suggested that 'we're so good at positive action that if you are white, male and middle-class you won't get in', there may well be a stage in the selection process when the balance of the intake requires that preference be given to categories so far under-represented. Understandably, 'the idea that a child might improve his or her chances of being admitted by doing badly in the test was certainly a foreign one to many parents' (Murphy *et al.* 1990: 5). There is a real dilemma here which was apparently unperceived in the DES. If, for example, significantly more applications are received from boys than from girls, then securing a gender balance in the intake may require discrimination against boys which equal opportunities legislation would prohibit. Similarly, if there are so many suitable applications from ethnic minority groups that their representative 'share' is achieved early in the selection process, then subsequent applicants may be rejected largely on grounds of race.

Despite her objections to the Nottingham Report, Susan Fey herself noted some of these difficulties in the interview from which we have already quoted. She also emphasised, justifiably, the peculiar difficulties which CTCs face in explaining to disappointed parents the selection procedures they use.

If you are taking the cleverest, people may not like it but they understand it and accept it. If you say, we'll take the first come first served – ditto. If you say, we'll only take people whose brothers and sisters – you know, whatever you want to say, people understand these things and accept them even even if they don't like them. But to do what we're doing is so alien to the system here that it's very difficult to get across.

What was 'alien' was not selection as such, but selection on criteria other than academic merit. When Sir Cyril Taylor referred in interview to the 'embarrassing popularity' of CTCs, what might otherwise seem a curious comment by the programme's principal propagandist is comprehensible in the context of having to whittle the applications down through a process unusual in complexity and subtlety.

> CTCs could be among the most highly selective schools in the country. They could be technical grammar schools, which of course is exactly what some people say they should be. But we reject a hell of a lot of bright kids, which is a tragedy, but we have to keep to the law.

What the law requires is an intake appropriately stratified in ability and social composition. We turn now to how CTCs have tried to meet that requirement.

SELECTION AND CHOICE

In presenting CTCs as a new 'choice' of secondary school, both the DES and the CTC Trust have had to avoid drawing attention to the extent to which it is the schools which do the choosing. In an ideal matching of supply and demand, something like 180 suitable applicants would emerge from the selection process so that none meeting the individual criteria relating to aptitude and commitment is denied admission, and all the categories required by the obligation to be 'representative' are filled. Yet demand has considerably exceeded supply. If that was anticipated by the DES, then the process of selection should have received more careful attention than it did.

We have avoided equating CTCs too simply with magnet schools. But in relation to securing socially 'balanced' intakes, they face similar difficulties. The US versions of specialised high schools are intended to exert a magnetic pull across the usual boundaries of race and class, thereby enabling distinctive forms of educational excellence to be achieved in socially disadvantaged areas. Ideally, parents' choice of specialisation should be so dispersed across a wide range of alternatives that each attracts on its distinctive merits a socially mixed intake. But while it can be claimed that many magnet schools are more accessible to disadvantaged groups than are either neighbourhood schools in 'superior' neighbourhoods or those suburban schools which are 'mostly open only to white families and calibrated to their income' (Metz 1990: 114), the demand for others is so high that they can avoid recruiting students they regard as being academic risks or potential trouble (Blank 1990). In the context of English secondary education, with its long tradition of withholding parity of esteem for alternative versions, it is perhaps especially unlikely that a 'new kind of school' will be perceived simply as different but equal and so attract applications only from parents and pupils with a particular interest in the distinctive curriculum being offered.

Being untried and overtly innovative, the initial challenge facing CTCs was to fill their places and so avoid the embarrassment of a 'new choice of school' being insufficiently in demand. Although the controversy surrounding them ensured continuing media attention, a DES-commissioned survey in 1989 showed that two-thirds of a large sample of those sampled had not heard of CTCs at all. Among 'classes' C2–E, the obvious target groups given the programme's inner-city orientation, that figure was as high as 77 per cent. Many of those aware that CTCs existed thought either that they were for 'high-ability pupils only', or that they could take children from anywhere within reasonable travelling distance.[3] The sample was drawn, however, from electoral wards across the country, few of which would have had a CTC visible or in prospect. Where CTCs have emerged, political hostility and the opposition of local interest groups has usually elicited heavy and prolonged coverage in local media. Once established, most CTCs have had the appeal of new buildings, a high-tech and distinctly modern image, apparently lavish resources, and the promise of occupational advantages arising from unusually close links with sponsors and other local employers. They are located, if their promoters and project directors are believed, in areas where maintained secondary schools are widely perceived as having failed. They are also likely to include among their sponsors people well practised in marketing new products to a wide range of potential customers.

For these reasons, and despite the obstacles to publicising themselves in potential 'feeder' schools created in some areas by LEA hostility, most CTCs have been oversubscribed from the start. For the school year beginning in September 1991, there were 8,065 applications for the 2,553 places offered by thirteen

CTCs. As reported by the CTC Trust (1991a: 6), the ratio of applications to places ranged from 4.4 at Bacon's and Haberdashers' and 4.0 at Dixon's to 2.1 at Djanogly and 1.8 at Leigh. Such apparent differences in popularity obviously reflect local circumstances and the nature of the competition as well as a CTC's emerging reputation. Leigh for example, which had the lowest ratio of demand to supply, is in competition with some of Kent's remaining grammar schools and is hampered by the residual reputation of the 'secondary modern' comprehensive which it replaced and by being refurbished rather than built anew. Unlike other CTCs, it has a number of its offers of places rejected if a more conventional route to 'good' secondary education becomes available and had little scope for choice in its first year. Bacon's has inherited the reputation of a voluntary-aided comprehensive with strong residues of the grammar school it had previously been. In new buildings, it is also the only school within a two-mile radius of its Docklands setting and most of its intake come from a densely populated (and multi-ethnic) area between the Old Kent Road and the Thames. As its principal commented to us, local people 'are desperate to get into what they are considering their local school, whereas the CTC programme is all about catchment areas'. The Performing Arts and Technology School is the only one of its kind, and attracted 1,300 applications for its 300 places in 1991. Djanogly and Macmillan, each taking its third intake in 1991, claimed to have deliberately dampened demand to avoid disappointing too many of those who had applied and to make their selection process more manageable. Each claimed to have welcomed a drop in applications between 1990 and 1991. Kingshurst's principal, however, took pride in claiming 1,000 applications for its places for 1991, interpeting that figure as meaning that most 'eligible' parents in the catchment area now apply to the CTC.[4]

Such popularity may be good for a CTC's self-esteem, but it leads to expensive and time-consuming selection processes which often include but go far beyond the formal testing of ability. Unless the relevant information is routinely provided for all potential entrants by LEAs or feeder schools, and hostility to CTCs makes this unlikely in most areas, then standardised tests must be used to establish the 'wide range of ability' required by the government's intake criteria. Their use is then likely to heighten the difficulty of explaining to disappointed parents why their child has not been chosen by creating an obvious resemblance to the eleven-plus and its private sector equivalents even though the actual process is much more complex than a simple order of academic merit. The original DES admissions criteria also referred to 'readiness to take advantage of the type of education offered in CTCs', thereby raising immediate objections to identifying specialised aptitudes at so early an age. Although some CTCs ask primary heads to identify the extent of a child's technical aptitude, the following comment by a project director reflects a degree of scepticism about such an exercise:

> We're charged with admitting children who have a kind of aptitude for a school with a technological bias. There is no way on this earth that anybody can take children at the age of 11 and determine unequivocally any kind of aptitude bias they have. And so I ignored it.

Qualitative evidence complements the base data provided by test scores. The interviewing of all applicants and their parents was initially required by the DES, and provides the opportunity to enquire into the child's enthusiasm for the CTC. One principal reported that if the parents seemed keen but the child was not, then he 'sided' with the child; if the child was keen but the parents were not, then he waited for some expression of real parental commitment. He also insisted that the test scores were used more as background information than as a selective filter and that he made it clear to parents that he was 'offering places to pupils, not to results'. Another principal emphasised that the parental interviews were 'two way', and that he used the occasion to warn parents about the longer school day and about the hostility they might encounter as a consequence of choosing the CTC; presumably to discourage all but the most committed from accepting places. A number of CTCs have used outsiders (usually retired headteachers and teachers) to do their interviewing, though several have decided to use their own staff instead because of the perceived benefits to their professional development.

The Nottingham study cited earlier was critical of interviewers' lack of training in what to look for, which created differences in the kinds of recommendations they made, and warned that 'the interview by definition tends to favour the

Table 4.1 Offers made to applicants to one CTC for entry at 11-plus (August 1991)

Stanines	National distribution (%)	CTC (%)	Ethnic minorities		Indigenous	
			Boys (N)	Girls (N)	Boys (N)	Girls (N)
1 (low)	4	4.7	1	3	1	3
2	7	10.6	3	3	5	7
3	12	17.1	6	10	8	5
4	17	25.3	13	8	14	8
5	20	14.7	3	6	10	6
6	17	15.3	6	3	12	5
7	12	7.1	1	1	2	8
8	7	4.1	3	1	3	–
9 (high)	4	1.1	–	–	1	1
	100	100	36	35	56	43

articulate' and so may act as a social filter (Murphy *et al.* 1990: 7). The CTCs we visited claimed to be anxious not to favour the persuasive, one safeguard being to separate the interviewing from deciding whom to admit. An internal report on the 1991 intake to one CTC noted that 'by far the greater proportion of the applicants' parents came from the lower range of the socio-economic scale', and that during selection this tendency was extended. There is no doubt that the commitment in some CTCs to securing a comprehensive intake goes well beyond meeting the formal requirements imposed by the DES, and reflects both their determination to demonstrate what can be achieved with such an intake and a recognition of the damage they would sustain if shown to be unfairly selective. Table 4.1 illustrates from one CTC the care taken in monitoring the ability range and representativeness of intakes across ethnic groups. However, there are considerable problems in interpreting the data made available by CTCs and it is often far from clear on what basis applicants are ascribed to particular categories.

The extent of the effort involved in securing representative intakes has brought suggestions that stratified random selection might be the most economical way of achieving the required balance. As Susan Fey put it:

> In other words, once you've got to the stage when you've got sufficient numbers in each category for the criteria, at that stage you use a random selection which is either done by a computer so it's totally objective or it's done by an outside body.

The notion that such a democratic lottery may provide the fairest method of selection has emerged in several 'magnetised' secondary school systems in the United States. Something like it may be adopted on principle and to economise on time, and at least one CTC has already used random selection to reduce the number of applicants to be interviewed.

We now consider how far CTCs generally are meeting the requirements imposed on them before describing, in the final sections of the chapter, some characteristics of the intakes to two particular CTCs.

Given the traditional substantial under-representation of girls in the subjects in which CTCs are expected to specialise, it is surprising that their considerable success in achieving balanced

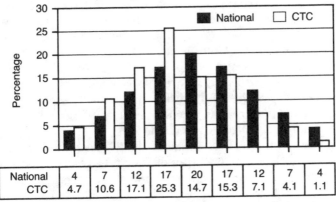

Distribution comparison
National values against one CTC's 1991 intake

National	4	7	12	17	20	17	12	7	4
CTC	4.7	10.6	17.1	25.3	14.7	15.3	7.1	4.1	1.1

Stanines

Based on 11-plus offers for August 1991

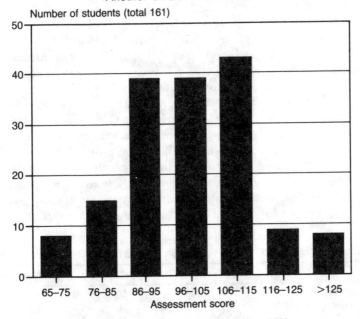

Another CTC's 1991 intake

Number of students (total 161)

Assessment score

Figure 4.1 The ability distribution of intakes to two CTCs

intakes has not been given more publicity by the Trust and by the government. Indeed, it is not explicitly mentioned in the Trust's 1991 progress report, although the front cover has a balanced line-up of three girls and three boys and its technology-related photographs of CTCs at work show a preponderance of girls. Of the eight CTCs for which we have detailed figures, four had roughly equal numbers of boys and girls across successive intakes if not in each year; in three of the others, girls represented 45–7 per cent of the 1991 entries. In the one exception to this rough equality, girls had been just below 40 per cent of the applications and of those admitted.

In relation to the 'wide range of ability' which intakes should display, the Nottingham study of four CTCs noted that while entrants' scores were around the national average for the various NFER tests being used, they were likely to have been 'well above those found in their respective catchment areas' (Murphy *et al.* 1990: 9). CTCs have tended either to display the ability range of their intakes by a simple comparison of average test scores, or by a more useful comparison of the distribution of scores across ability bands as is done by the two CTCs used as illustration in Figure 4.1.

Neither of those displays addresses the problem of how to compare the scores of those admitted to a CTC with the ability distribution in its catchment area. What CTCs have sometimes done, as is illustrated in Table 4.2, is to demonstrate that their intakes have been fairly representative of the ability of those who applied or have been deliberately skewed downwards. The example shown in Table 4.2 is taken from a CTC which had been especially anxious to show that contrary to local criticism, it had drawn both a higher than (national) average proportion from the lower ability bands and a higher proportion than it could have done given the range of ability among all those who had applied.

That second criterion may seem a reasonable test of good intentions, and can clearly be applied to the third constraint on

Table 4.2 Distribution of first-year intake across five ability bands (1991)

	A (low)	B	C	D	E (high)
National	10	20	40	20	10
Applicants to CTC	11	20	46	17	6
Admissions to CTC	13	24	41	18	4

intakes – that they should be representative of the social and ethnic character of the area. For if the data needed to establish representativeness in those respects are very unlikely to be available, then the CTC can only demonstrate that those whom it admits are a fair cross-section of those who applied. Again, the efforts to avoid being or seeming socially selective have sometimes been strenuous. They should also be put in the context of application rates high enough in at least some cases to enable the CTC to be, as Sir Cyril Taylor remarked to us, 'among the most selective schools in the country'. In practice, the claim made by one CTC that the 'vast majority' of its intakes 'will be working-class or lower middle-class' seems largely borne out by the limited data available. However, given the nature of the CTC 'mission', the CTC Trust might have been expected to monitor intake characteristics across all the CTCs more systematically than has been done. One CTC claimed that more than half its 1991 intake came from 'very highly' or 'highly' deprived backgrounds; several emphasised the extent to which they positively discriminated in favour of applicants from the 'poorest' parts of their catchment area; and one, treating the length of parents' full-time education as 'the most dependable indicator of socio-economic status', reported that 63 per cent had left at or before the age of 16. Thus, the categories employed are inconsistent and the definitions adopted vary considerably. Nevertheless, a working-class/lower-middle-class majority has certainly been apparent at the first CTC (Walford and Miller 1991: 112–16; Gewirtz et al. 1991). Ethnic 'representativeness' will obviously create significant differences between CTCs, several of which (for example, Emmanuel, Macmillan and Corby) are in areas with small minority ethnic populations. Even where that is the case, CTCs tend to claim an over-representation of pupils from Asian and Afro-Caribbean backgrounds, while several others do so while also being able to claim proportions in their 1991 intakes as high as 30 per cent at Harris and 42 per cent at Djanogly. However, it is not always clear whether the overall figures for minority ethnic groups conceal an over-representation or under-representation of particular ethnic minorities. It is also impossible to tell how far the ethnic minority children accepted are representative of the minority ethnic population as a whole in terms of their social class backgrounds.

The difficulty of securing representativeness may be considerable, at least initially. It can be illustrated briefly from the experience of one CTC, the first intake to which was strongly criticised for its selectiveness. As the chief education officer commented to us, 'while the location is inner-city, the reality is that three-quarters of the pupils come from schools in the posh quarter'. The CTC's project director thought that judgement not inaccurate, and could see advantages in having a 'good' first intake which could 'set the tone for the school'. But he also remarked that all they were offering when the first applications were being invited was 'a building site and a promise, and who but the middle class would buy that!' There were then too few applicants to give scope for managing the intake, and so few from the poorest parts of the catchment area that (as one of its teachers remarked) 'if you couldn't read, you were in'. Publicity for the next intake was therefore targeted on those 'poorer' areas (excessively so, the project director thought), producing in the second year an intake which the principal described as being 'deliberately skewed towards the CTC mission' – that is, towards demonstrating what could be achieved with apparently unpromising material.

Where that 'mission' is accepted, it presents the challenge of how best to reach the kinds of children most in need of the 'fresh opportunities' which CTCs see themselves as providing. It is the challenge which our previous research suggested that the Assisted Places Scheme had not overcome. We reported that while most place-holders in our sample came from 'less well-off homes', very few came from the kinds of culturally disadvantaged backgrounds that had figured prominently in the scheme's rhetoric of legitimation. We also found little evidence of such children being given preference, once they had met a school's academic entry criteria, over abler children from less disadvantaged backgrounds (Edwards et al. 1989). Reviewing that book, the then chairman of the Headmasters' Conference saw our findings 'as a challenge rather than a condemnation', the challenge being that independent schools had to 'try harder to reach those parents and children who have always had most to gain from education as a ladder'.[5]

Leading independent schools are accustomed to wait for parents to come to them. CTCs have to create their market, and some sponsors displayed a strong obligation not to recruit only or mainly 'clever kids, and well-intentioned, well-motivated parents who would make the school a roaring success'. That comment from the main sponsor of a northern CTC preceded his firmly declared intention to reach the children 'who need the school most' but who were also likely to be from homes unpractised in perceiving new opportunities. The fact that he and other sponsors 'are marketing people, that's what we're good at', gave them in his view the experience in selling new products which could overcome traditional parental inertia in an area with very low staying-on rates. Denied direct access to local primary schools by the LEA, their publicity campaign used leaflets 'with lots of pictures, easy to read, delivered door-to-door', stands in local supermarkets, a 'livery van doing the rounds', and a willingness on their part and of the principal-designate to speak to 'anyone, anywhere'. Another of that CTC's sponsors described the intake it was seeking as 'a good mix, both of ability and background, but with substantial numbers from 'the more deprived and depressed areas of [the city]'. That is the 'mix' which CTCs generally have claimed.

Statistical demonstrations of the representativeness of CTC intakes are unlikely to be sufficient in themselves. Thus one director of education, while admitting that the local CTC met the quantitative tests on ability and socio-economic status, went on to comment:

> But they're getting well-motivated pupils with supportive families. You've got to be a bit of a stayer to go through the process of choice. . . . It's a powerful process of self-selection, and the resulting pupils and parents are unlikely to be typical.

A similar comment was made by Andrew Turner, director of the Grant Maintained Schools Trust, when he suggested that whereas a school opting out would retain its present character, a CTC will 'change its intake to people with a particular attitude or commitment' (quoted in Hammer and Flude 1989: 377). What is unusual (though not unique) about the selection process is the explicit assessment of family suitability. Denying initially any intention of reviving the eleven-plus, Kenneth Baker emphasised the importance of pupil and parental attitudes, and of 'the motivation to succeed to the limits of the individual's capacity' (quoted in the *New Scientist* 16 October 1986). The inclusion of parents in the interviewing of applicants provides an opportunity to enquire into attitudes which have traditionally acted as a substantial social filter – notably a willingness to support prolonged full-time education and training and a belief in 'qualities of enterprise, self-reliance and reponsibility'. Such a filter is seen by Roger Dale (1990) as extending the definition of 'merit' so as to exclude those (of whatever 'ability') who might waste a place because they lack a family background endowed with attitudes strategic for educational success. That approach was clearly articulated by a main sponsor of one CTC:

> Well, we are looking for children, during the testing and during the interviewing, who have an enthusiasm, who have an ability to benefit from the sort of education we are offering, who have parents who would be supportive of the college, both in ensuring that the children do the homework that's necessary, who will be part of the college life so that when we have activities the parents will be out in force. . . . So it's ability to benefit from what's on offer, and a willingness to be involved.

Such parents may be very untypical of the ethnic or social class 'quota' to which statistically they contribute. That possibility has shaped the more detailed analysis which follows of the grounds on which children and parents had sought a place at two CTCs.

REASONS FOR CHOOSING A CTC

Kingshurst CTC in Solihull and Harris CTC in Croydon represent two different models of CTC development in that Kingshurst was started from scratch in 1988, albeit in a redundant and refurbished school building, while Harris took a first-year CTC intake into the school in 1990 to join four years of pupils recruited when it was the LEA-maintained Sylvan High School.

The evidence we present comes mainly from interviews with thirty-eight parents and eighty-eight students (we have used the term strongly preferred to pupils by most CTCs), drawn in equal numbers from the two CTCs. They have been given pseudonyms whenever cited or quoted. All of them had both chosen Kingshurst or Harris and had themselves been chosen. Although we came across some unsuccessful applicants to CTCs in our interviews in other local schools, they were too few to make any useful inferences about applicants who had been rejected.

Although school choice is often considered a matter for parents, there were few instances where the decision seemed to have been theirs alone and Michelle (Harris) was unusual in explaining that 'there are no really good schools around and my mum wanted me to try it'. Most students had been actively involved in the process of choosing, and in some cases their voice had been decisive. In previous research, we had 'observed that parents determined to send their children to private schools were rather more inclined to press their choice on unwilling children than were parents with children in the state sector (Edwards *et al.* 1989: 213–14). In this respect, our CTC sample were more like the latter. The students often seemed to know more about the CTC than their parents and it was sometimes they who had been instrumental in breaking out of the conventional mould. Thus Mrs Cole (Kingshurst) reported of her daughter,

> It was her own idea. . . . We had this leaflet come through the door. We didn't take much notice. . . . It was all Rebecca's doing. I think they went round the school, didn't they, a caravan or something. . . . We would have chosen —— school, it's close and the two boys went there. . . . It was really Rebecca's decision, not ours.

The novelty of CTCs seemed to have made publicity leaflets and meetings more important than usual in prompting or shaping school choice, especially where LEAs had requested primary schools not to offer advice or information about entry to a CTC and before parental grapevines had had time to develop as an informal source of guidance. That the standard of presentation was generally high may reflect the influence of sponsors experienced in marketing, though one such sponsor warned that a glossiness 'more akin to a sales brochure for a computer software firm' might well deter the very people his CTC was trying to reach.

Some of those we interviewed had clearly been attracted by promises of a new kind of secondary education, like Jonathan who had read the Kingshurst booklet and thought, 'This is my future, and I really wanted to come here and get a good job out of it'. But the reasons we were given for preferring a CTC were no more often a straightforward choice of a distinctively technological form of secondary education than a reflection of more general factors found in recent studies of school choice (Adler *et al.* 1989; Coldron and Boulton 1991). At Harris, the fact that the school was already running as Sylvan meant that many students had chosen it for reasons apparently unconnected with its new status as a CTC. Indeed, several continued to refer to it by its former name, and there were frequent references to such traditional factors as proximity, past reputation, or the presence of siblings or friends. Thus Keith 'would have come to Sylvan anyway', and Diane 'wanted to go to Sylvan because my sister went to Sylvan and I wanted to go because it was a good school'. For Jason, who 'only lived up the road', it was 'the closest school around . . . any other school, I'd have had to catch buses'.

There were other Harris students, however, who, like almost all those we interviewed at Kingshurst, gave reasons which reflected some of the distinctive advantages which CTCs claim. The following responses indicate the importance of technology in the choice of a CTC:

> It was new and it had a lot of technology in it, and I was told that I'd have a better chance with using new equipment. (Kevin, Kingshurst)

> Yes, because I'd be able to know more about technology and have a better future. (Stuart, Kingshurst)

> Very important. I wanted to find out about computing and other technology. (Matthew, Kingshurst)

> I like working with computers and I thought it would be a challenge. (Elizabeth, Harris)

> It sounded good. There was going to be a lot more technology here than other schools. (Paul, Harris)

At Harris, the school's technological image seemed to be the dominant CTC-specific factor. This was less marked at Kingshurst. Walford has noted from his own interviews there the 'unexpected' finding that 'less than a quarter of the responses were about computing, science and technology aspects of the CTC' (Walford 1991b: 72; Walford and Miller 1991: 89–99). He suggests that rather than the CTC having a distinct clientele with an orientation towards technology, students tended to see the CTC in more general terms as offering a 'better education' and access to 'better' jobs. In our own interviews, an unspecified sense of having access to unusual opportunities was also strong.

> Well, there isn't any other school that is as good as this, and I just wanted to see if I could get into it. (Jonathan, Kingshurst)

> 'Cos I thought it had a good education so I'd get a good job afterwards. (Shane, Harris)

> 'Cos I wanted to be a electrician or something to do with electronics, so I thought it might be easier to go to a CTC school. (Guy, Harris)

For some students, the novelty of the CTC had been a factor, providing a welcome contrast to the prevailing images of other schools:

> Technology was all right, but it was that it was a new school. (Maurice, Kingshurst)

> It was just that it was different from other schools that I wanted to come here. (Colin, Kingshurst)

> It was more that the other schools that I've seen are nearly falling down, and this place is all new. (Kevin, Kingshurst)

We complete our illustration of students' various explanations of their choice with three from Harris. Tariq 'just felt proud coming to a college instead of a proper secondary school'; Melanie had thought 'it sounded really good – a new school, a good idea what with all the computers – and I get bored in the holidays anyway'; and Nigel explained that his parents 'had split up and my father wouldn't pay any more for the private school I'd been going to because of my dyslexia'. The existence of the specialised dyslexia unit at Harris, which caters for about 10 per cent of the intake, was mentioned as a significant factor by four of the students we spoke to.

Although the student voice seemed often to have carried weight, parents had their own priorities which sometimes resembled and sometimes diverged from those of their children. At Harris, we again found cases where the reasons for choosing it seemed unrelated to its new status and even to reflect an assumption that little had changed from its previous existence. Thus Mrs Raines chose it 'mainly because his sister was already here [at Sylvan] and we were pleased with how she had got on'. But there were also many references to what were seen as unusually extensive IT provision and unusually close links with business and industry.

> Although Sylvan had a bad name, I had seen a documentary on Solihull CTC and I liked the link with business and the computers. It's the thing of the future. (Mrs Wall, Harris)

> The promise of all the new technology. (Mr Mallen, Harris)

> He's going to need a good education to get anywhere in this world and he's interested in computers. (Mrs Vole, Harris)

> The CTC seemed a good idea. I think he needs a technical school. (Mr Miller, Kingshurst)

What was less predictable was the frequency with which parents also stressed the attraction of a style or standard of secondary education which they believed was no longer generally available in the locality. In making this point, they were understandably more likely than their children to make comparisons with other schools:

> I read the booklet and decided that the ideas contained in the booklet had a good basis and we were looking to the future. We were a bit disappointed with the school that Richard went to and we felt we could get more for Rachel if she was able to go there. . . . She would have gone to —— if she hadn't gone to the CTC, because . . . it's the only school in the area that has certain standards. The others have got even less. (Mrs Hunter, Kingshurst)

> We looked at all the schools. The elder one was at —— and it didn't stretch him really. —— is really run-down. So it was really a lack of choice in the vicinity. (Mrs Wall, Harris)

> We thought it might be good because it was a new system . . . different from other schools and I liked that it was more technical than others. (Mrs Haq, Harris)

In drawing such contrasts, parents often mentioned the distinctive ethos to which CTC prospectuses draw attention as the context for their modern facilities. Thus Mrs Fry had believed that Harris CTC would be 'more structured than some of the other schools', and Mr Duncan that it would demand 'commitment from parents from the start and that was what we wanted'.

Over half the Harris parents we interviewed were highly critical of comprehensive schools, and often regretted the passing of grammar schools even when they had no direct experience of them. Most others were at best ambivalent about the practice of comprehensive education. What was notable was how few agreed with Mrs Anthony in regarding Harris CTC itself as 'a comprehensive school really'. Most drew a contrast with comprehensive schools, even when they had difficulty in defining the differences beyond the assumption that it offered a 'better' education.

Maintained grammar schools had virtually disappeared from the area around Harris, but in Birmingham they remained an alternative for parents of academically able children. Just under half of the parents interviewed at Kingshurst said they had considered a grammar school for their child. None had actually refused an offer of a grammar school place to attend Kingshurst, although Sean had resisted his parents' persuasion to take the entrance examination for King Edward's Grammar School because 'I just thought this one would be better – with all the new technology they're putting in'. Half the parents declared themselves strongly in favour of grammar schools. Although a few regarded them as too exclusive, and preferred a CTC for that reason, it was more usual either to place the CTC near the top of the local hierarchy of schools or to be uncertain about its status in relation to Birmingham's grammar schools.

> Grammar schools – I think that was the next best thing to the CTC. I think you can class the CTC just like that, as a grammar school. (Mrs Ingram)

> I think a certain type of child from a certain background goes to the Birmingham grammar schools. ... The CTC's still selective the same as the grammar schools but they have a wider variety, they're sort of more liberal than the grammar school selection. (Mrs Cutler)

> There's not many people like our families that get in unless they are extremely clever. (Mrs Shields)

> Obviously, it [the grammar school] was the best thing around until the CTC. There again, you always got the best teachers. (Mr Smith)

Some parents also compared CTCs with private schools. While most of those we interviewed, from both CTCs, thought that private education was better than that offered at state schools, only a few regarded it as within their means. For those who might have considered it, a CTC had sometimes seemed a welcome alternative. Mrs Madison (Harris) had heard about the CTC:

> It was supposed to be strong in the subjects he likes – computing, maths and sciences. . . . Otherwise, we only put church schools down because the state schools around here are horrendous. And he also took exams for scholarships. . . . He would have gone to —— or —— if he'd got a scholarship, but he wanted to go here because they had a computer for each pupil.

Mrs Martin (Kingshurst) 'couldn't believe our luck when she got in, because it's like getting a private education', and Mr Whittle (Harris) had been persuaded by what he saw as the CTC's similarity to a private school.

> All the things they were saying, the technology, that's the thing of future . . . it seemed to me to be a private school with no fees – only by what everyone was saying, Sir Philip Harris and all of them.

Asked later in the interview to identify what he liked about the CTC now that his son was there, he returned to his comparison though this time with some suggestion of an inferior version. 'That sort of school', he thought, 'can give more to the kids than other schools – unless you have the money. For the normal, working-class person, it's a good school'. Two Kingshurst parents argued that parents who had experienced the quality of the education there would now be willing to pay fees to maintain it. As Mr Cole put it, 'I should imagine we'd pay for like part funding or something like that if it ever occurred . . . say if like the Labour government come in, and stop the funding of it or something'.

Roger Dale has argued that CTCs are intended to 'facilitate a shift from collectivism to individualism, from a view that a common school is desirable to one that encourages parents/consumers to shop around and maximise their children's opportunities of enjoying an "uncommon" education' (Dale 1990:

9–10; see also Gewirtz *et al.* 1991). The views we have cited seem to support that interpretation, though 'individualism' may have been well established before CTCs were 'created' to encourage it. Some parents, however, seemed to feel a certain 'collectivist' guilt about their choice, to lay more emphasis on the CTC's state funding than on its independence, and to admit some conflict between getting 'the best' for their own children and wanting 'the best' for all children:

> Well, this is hypocritical, very hypocritical, because the CTC is a Conservative venture and we don't agree with it at all. I mean we felt very hypocritical sending Craig to the CTC when we didn't agree with none of its policies. We thought if secondary schools had the same amount of money and the same amount of publicity they could be just as good and it's wrong that 180 out of 2,000 applicants can get in. (Mrs Donald, Kingshurst)

> I weren't going to send her in the beginning because I didn't agree with it. . . . I think it should be available in every school. I thought they was being choosy. . . . I think they should all be as good as the CTC but they're not. (Mrs Truman, Kingshurst)

> It's got everything that a young person would need for a good education, as long as they take advantage of it, of course. All schools should be like Harris and it's sad that a lot of schools are deprived of computers and other equipment. (Mrs Sage, Harris)

Mr Herbert (Kingshurst) justified his child's CTC place on the grounds that CTCs would ultimately benefit others if they were

> part of an experiment into widening the choice in education. . . . If they were just creating a series of schools where three or four times the amount of money were spent on pupils for the sake of doing it, then I would disapprove of them I think.

More generally, and despite strong criticism of comprehensive schools and of their underfunding, the fact that CTCs were independent of LEAs was a significant attraction to only a small minority of the parents we interviewed. The following comment is vivid, but untypical:

I think they [schools] should all be independent of the council anyway, 'cos half the teachers are frightened to say boo to a goose because of the different councils and God knows what else. . . . I don't think the comprehensive system works. I mean, if it works, why are all these comprehensive schools opting out? (Mrs Martin, Kingshurst)

Independence from LEA control as such seemed to be significant for parents from only one of the five LEAs (three of them Labour-controlled) from which Harris drew its students. That one LEA had often been targeted in the tabloid press as an example of 'loony Left' incompetence.

CHARACTERISTICS OF CTC INTAKES

Given the 'unworkability' of the DES entry requirements, and the fact that both Kingshurst and Harris CTCs have been considerably oversubscribed, we examined their intakes to see whether they justify the suspicion of critics that CTCs will be both academically and socially selective. Our evidence has necessarily been drawn from the CTCs themselves, although it has been supplemented for Harris by data provided by one of the local LEAs.

We described earlier the difficulty even of defining the ability distribution against which CTC intakes should be measured. The first intake to Kingshurst, as reported by Walford and Miller (1991), had an average IQ score of 98 which compared with an average of around 90 for north Solihull as a whole. The lack of similar figures for east Birmingham makes the catchment area test impossible to apply, though it seems likely that the scores were above the average for the districts from which the CTC drew its students. The second intake had an average IQ score of 96.4 after the catchment area had been adjusted to create a better 'balance'. The method of selecting students at Kingshurst ensured that, as far as possible, the intake was representative of applicants and distributed on a normal curve. However, given that the analysis of test results is done by stanines, reference to other criteria could lead to selection of those pupils at the top of each stanine – a criticism which has been made of how Church schools in London often used the ILEA's much broader banding system. Nevertheless, it would be difficult to argue, on the basis of these figures, that the Kingshurst intake is markedly 'able'.

The extent to which the intake to Harris was representative of its catchment area was also difficult to ascertain, although Croydon LEA analysed the characteristics of the sixty students admitted to Harris from its primary schools in 1991 on the same basis as it analysed the intakes to its own secondary schools. These analyses showed that the curve of distribution for the first intake was slightly skewed upwards in mathematics scores and slightly downwards in English. The CTC staff used these data, and their own figures on the total intake in relation to applicants, to make adjustments to their intake procedures for the second intake. Again, there was no evidence of the intakes to Harris being unusually weighted with academically 'able' children, and there were certainly maintained comprehensive schools within its feeder LEAs that received more academically able intakes.

Data on the social backgrounds of students at Kingshurst and Harris have been derived from our own pupil questionnaires and interviews, and details of the social class backgrounds of Kingshurst and Harris students are summarised in Table 4.3.

These first intakes showed no evidence of a middle-class bias, despite the presence of significant numbers of non-manual workers among the parents at Harris. In fact, the social class composition of these CTC intakes corresponded closely to that of the local population and local comprehensive schools. That

Table 4.3 Social class of parents of first-year intake students at two CTCs (rounded percentages)

	I	II	IIIN	IIIM	IV	V	Unemployed	Homeworker
Kingshurst (1988 intake)								
Fathers	1	9	12	49	21	2	6	0
Mothers	0	9	45	4	16	3	7	16
Harris (1990 intake)								
Fathers	9	17	17	23	20	3	11	0
Mothers	0	26	20	6	9	11	6	15

Source: Based on a sample of pupil interviews and questionnaires (N = 155) and classified according to OPCS social class classification (Office of Population Censuses and Surveys 1980)

this contrasts sharply with our earlier findings about the Assisted Places Scheme (Edwards *et al.* 1989) may indicate both the broader appeal of CTCs and the experience of CTC sponsors in marketing goods and services to a diverse population. Nevertheless, given the prominence of the inner-city mission assigned to CTCs, we find it extraordinary that the CTC Trust's own monitoring of the social composition of intakes is so light and unsystematic.

We therefore explored the backgrounds of CTC parents in rather more detail during interviews with parents broadly representative of the larger student sample in terms of social class and ethnicity. Some of the results of this necessarily limited inquiry are presented in Table 4.4

There is certainly no evidence at Kingshurst of a group of

Table 4.4 Education of parents of students at two CTCs

	Kingshurst		Harris	
	Fathers	Mothers	Fathers	Mothers
School type				
Elementary/secondary modern	10	13	4	6
Technical	0	1	0	0
Grammar	3	1	3	5
Comprehensive	4	4	3	3
State school overseas	0	0	2	2
Private (UK)	0	0	1	1
Private (overseas)	0	0	3	2
No data	2	0	3	0
School leaving age				
14	1	1	0	0
15	4	8	4	4
16	11	7	4	9
17	2	1	1	3
18-plus	0	2	6	2
No data	1	0	4	1
Highest qualification from school				
None	8	12	5	8
CSEs	3	5	1	0
GCE O-levels/School Certificate	5	2	3	6
GCE A-levels/Higher School Certificate	0	0	5	2
Other	0	0	1	2
No data	3	0	4	1

Source: Based upon data from nineteen parental interviews at Kingshurst and nineteen parental interviews at Harris

parents rich in educational and cultural capital. Most had been to non-selective secondary schools, only five had stayed on in full-time education beyond 16, and more than half had left school with no formal qualifications. Many more Harris parents had attended selective schools and seven of them had received a private education. They also tended to have left school later and with higher level qualifications, seven having obtained A-levels or their equivalent. Of the whole sample, about half had gained qualifications after leaving school – mostly GCE, City and Guilds, and Royal Society of Arts (RSA) qualifications by part-time study. Only six of the parents, all at Harris, had degree level qualifications.

To some extent, differences between Kingshurst and Harris are consistent with the different social class composition of their catchment areas and their intakes. The much higher proportion of minority ethnic students at Harris – over 40 per cent compared with around 5 per cent at Kingshurst – may also be significant. Most of those Harris parents who had stayed longer at school and obtained school certificate and higher school certificate qualifications had done so at state or private schools in the so-called New Commonwealth countries. The majority of the degree holders also came from such backgrounds. Although, in many cases, such parents occupied jobs in the British labour market that are usually associated with lower level qualifications, they retained higher aspirations for their children. CTCs may be particularly attractive to this fraction of the minority ethnic population, though perhaps less for their 'modern' facilities than for conforming to some traditional views of what a good school should offer. Mr and Mrs Hurn, an Afro-Caribbean couple educated in Guyana, had read the Harris prospectus and

> were impressed, because both my husband and I went to private schools and we expected a high level of output from Alick because he has ability.

For Mr Asif, an Asian with an Afro-Caribbean wife, Harris offered an acceptable alternative to the former direct-grant grammar school that his son had failed to get into, though he still felt that 'they could be worked a bit harder in terms of what they do in class and the homework could be a bit harder'.

Mrs Husain, from Pakistan and a trained teacher herself, was happier that the school conformed to her expectations:

> I hear from Tariq they are strict. I like that, I think they are
> quite disciplined ... I think they are working hard and
> they make the students work hard because Tariq always
> complains.

That such examples include both Asian and Afro-Caribbean
parents calls into question the stereotypes implicit in some
predictions that CTCs would attract only Asian students from
the minority ethnic population.

But even substantial evidence from the initial intakes to CTCs
should be treated with caution. The strong competition for
places that is now developing in most CTCs makes it difficult to
predict what form selection will take in the future and what
effects this will have on less advantaged groups. Furthermore,
on the basis of their own observations at Kingshurst, Walford
and Miller (1991) argue that CTCs will undoubtedly sponsor
some members of the working class (or the 'deserving poor' as
they once might have been called) out of their environment, but
that they will have little positive impact on that environment and
some negative consequences for those who remain in it. They
also argue that, as CTCs become increasingly popular, they will
wish to move up the traditional hierarchy of esteem, move to
more conventional curricular styles, and deviate from their
original role. In this connection, it may be significant that ADT,
one of the newer CTCs, was found by Wandsworth LEA to have
selected 'a high proportion of more able readers (37 per cent)
and a low proportion of less able readers (13 per cent)' and to
have the highest mean London Reading Test score of any
secondary school in the borough.[6] We discuss this issue further
in chapter 6, when considering where CTCs will fit into an
emergent hierarchy of schools.

Having explored student and parent expectations of CTCs,
and the characteristics which had led them to apply, we turn
now to the schools themselves and to those directions in which
their acceptance of a 'mission' to be innovative are leading them.

Chapter 5

Centres of innovation?

The promotion of city technology colleges as 'a new choice of school' carried a promise that they would be both excellent and different. While it was clearly essential that they should be good enough to show what could be achieved in apparently unpromising circumstances, they were also placed under an obligation to be something more than successful urban comprehensive schools. If the uniformity of existing secondary education was a prime cause of its mediocrity, as the government argued, then radical departures from it were urgently required. It was therefore for the general good of the system that CTCs would be 'pioneering new teaching methods, new ways of managing schools, and new approaches to technology and science'.[1]

The innovations promised in 1986 were a 'strong technical and practical element' in the curriculum, unusually extensive IT provision, and unusually direct contacts with business and industry (DES 1986). It was not clear how educationally different CTCs were intended to be beyond that remit. The notion of pilot schools set free for innovation in the hope that their example would spread goes back to the 'Young schools' contemplated at the launching of TVEI. Yet it would have been a marked departure from previous official caution towards unconventional secondary schooling if CTCs had indeed been given, as one of their principals claimed, 'a blank sheet' on which to write their plans (Andrews 1991). It would also have been politically risky. There were no grounds for believing that conspicuously unconventional schooling would be popular with parents, CTCs had to win a place in the market very quickly, and any signs of failure were certain to be used by their many detractors. They had at least to be 'good' schools, even if they had also to be more than that.

Any assessment of their educational quality must wait, whatever performance indicators are used, until they have complete intakes and until several cohorts of students have been through the test of public examination. Even then, for reasons given in chapter 6, controlled and fair comparisons with other kinds of schools will be difficult. In this chapter we therefore concentrate on early indications of how different CTCs are becoming.

Those heading them were certainly attracted by what they saw as exceptional opportunities for educational 'pioneering'. Djanogly's principal has defined as the CTCs' 'central brief' an obligation to 'take a fresh look at what might be done by way of useful innovation in the management of an inner-city comprehensive school' (Andrews 1991). Other principals, in this respect very much the organic intellectuals of the CTC 'movement', have described their task as being to experiment with 'radical and accelerated alternatives' to conventional secondary schooling, and to be 'the research and development arm of national education'.[2]

Although modernity and experimentation cannot be taken as synonymous, institutional self-presentation as 'schools of the future' is certainly prominent in CTC prospectuses and other public declarations of intent. Thus Emmanuel's first newsletter to prospective parents promised 'a new concept in educational thinking', supporting the assertion with references to new buildings, the 'latest equipment', a curriculum directly relevant to what employers wanted, and consequently enhanced prospects of employment. Corby CTC is described in an early promotional newsletter (July 1990) as 'designed to take advantage of latest developments in education and building design' and so as offering 'genuine alternatives' to conventional provision. Dixon's prospectus promises 'the school of the future', Djanogly's 'a school for tomorrow in Nottingham today', Thomas Telford's a 'high-tech school for the twenty-first century', and Macmillan's 'the very latest computers, computer software and high technology apparatus which your child will use from Day One'. Kingshurst backs its claim that 'the future has arrived for education beyond 16' with references to its possession of the most modern IT resources, and Leigh promises 'to meet and go beyond the challenge of tomorrow' by using 'the very latest equipment and teaching techniques' to open up 'whole new areas of learning' to its students.

Such open enthusiasm for innovation is apparently in keeping with Kenneth Baker's wish to see 'points of creative energy' inserted into a complacent, failing system. But the matter is more complicated than that. While Baker believed strongly in the motivating effects of a more technological and practical curriculum, and in the transforming effects of IT on learning, much of the political support for his initiative came from those eager to support a challenge to the LEA 'monopoly' rather than bold experiments with the content or process of secondary schooling. From that perspective, what was significant about CTCs was their funding and management. Indeed, some supporters of an open market assumed that greater consumer choice would strengthen the traditional forms of secondary schooling which they hoped to preserve or restore.

In our many interviews and conversations with CTC staff, however, as distinct from some with project directors and sponsors, we detected no sympathy with the initiative's political objectives beyond a belief that more radical and rapid changes could be made than had seemed feasible in an LEA setting. In our view, the ambition to be 'research and development' schools, licensed and enabled to take educational risks, has developed within the 'CTC movement' and represents something of an 'educationist' take-over of an otherwise highly politicised initiative. Being at 'the leading edge of change' in curriculum and pedagogy was clearly seen as a much more attractive role than that of piloting a break-up of the existing system of educational provision. One principal expressed his anxiety that the programme might be driven too hard by its initial objectives, with CTCs being 'slotted into a rag-bag of ideas which are often political styles or concepts of industry'. That anxiety was clearly shared by senior staff in other CTCs, as was his wish to see instead 'an educational philosophy . . . at the heart of the movement'.

It is of course a commonplace in policy analysis that implementation rarely proceeds according to plan because policymakers must hand over that task to 'agents' whose activities they cannot entirely channel and who may well have agendas of their own. In the case of CTCs, the initial brief was so vaguely defined as to leave considerable scope for diversion and subversion.

CTCs were also created as 'independent' schools. At least ostensibly, they had therefore to be given considerable freedom to develop in their own ways though under the constraints imposed by having to secure their place in the market. An intriguing consequence of that relative autonomy is that some of the innovations in curriculum and learning being promoted in certain CTCs are not easily compatible with other government interventions. They also illustrate tensions within the policy discourse of the Right. We begin our detailed discussion, however, with those characteristics of CTCs which reflect the main political impetus behind the pilot network and which were intended to point forward to a radical restructuring of educational provision.

INNOVATIONS IN STATUS, FUNDING AND MANAGEMENT

The most obvious political attraction of CTCs was that they would constitute 'a distinct category of provision within the education system' (DES 1986: 9), the first instalment of 'Thatcher's third tier' of state-independent schools (Simon 1992: 56–71). At the time the programme was announced, discussions were already taking place within the DES, prompted and shaped by the Prime Minister's Policy Unit and by right-wing pressure groups, in preparation for reshaping the system in accordance with neo-liberal principles. These principles combined the moral advocacy of consumer choice with the conviction that subjecting schools to the full effects of that choice would lead inexorably to an improvement in educational standards (Edwards and Whitty 1992). Schools were to be freed from bureaucratic control so that they could provide the kind of education which parents wanted, and denied bureaucratic protection if they failed to find and maintain their place in the market. If the CTC programme was to be a significant move in that direction, then individual CTCs had to be given considerable autonomy. We therefore consider first the administrative framework within which they operate.

It was a clear political imperative that LEA control should not be replaced by close and detailed supervision from the DES, even though the government pays all a CTC's running costs and had paid most of its capital cost as well. Each CTC is owned by a charitable trust, and protected against a change in status by a contract between government and trustees which requires seven years' notice of such a change. Given that CTCs represented a distinctly new 'category of provision', it is not surprising that contracts proved very difficult to draw up, the first funding agreements going through more than ten drafts and only being formalised after the earliest CTCs had opened. Financial arrangements were complex, and sponsors like Hanson and BAT brought in their own expert advisers to dispute some of the Treasury's assumptions. The final agreement also had to confirm the CTC's distinctive curriculum and the 'representativeness' of its intakes, establish the position of the trustees and the financial accountability of the governing body, and accept the secretary of state's responsibility for monitoring its educational performance. But although responsibility for the whole programme was explicitly assigned to the secretary of state in a ministerial division of labour which reflected Kenneth Baker's personal interest in the initiative,[3] DES supervision has been neither intrusive nor wide-ranging and it is not easy to see in the small CTC unit at the DES a significant part of that new 'focus of power' which Brian Simon (1992) identifies as an administrative consequence of 'Thatcher's third tier' of schools. Although we note later in chapter 6 some complaints from CTCs about DES slowness and inflexibility, we recorded no feeling that they had exchanged one master for another.

If CTCs were to demonstrate what could be achieved by giving schools the freedom to make their own decisions, it was also essential that the CTC Trust should not grow into a substitute LEA. As described in chapter 3, the Trust was formed in 1987 mainly to co-ordinate and accelerate the finding of sponsors and sites. Like the Grant-Maintained Schools Trust established in July 1988 and which initially shared the same building, it was also to provide a group of new schools with advice which, though informed by DES briefing, would be independent of the government (Hammer and Flude 1989). But the scope of its activities was considerably extended in 1989 by the creation of a Curriculum Development Unit, funded partly by firms wanting to support the CTC programme without being identified with particular CTCs and partly from a matching grant of about £200,000 from the DES on the understanding that the unit would become self-financing after four years. In its written bid for DES support, the Trust emphasised the value of a body which could support and disseminate innovations appropriate to 'the particular CTC mission' which would also benefit 'the whole of the secondary sector'. But it was also careful to emphasise too the importance of demonstrating how 'high quality secondary education' could be delivered 'without the top-heavy and often stultifying staffing structure of an LEA'.

Those two objectives are not easily aligned. Susan Fey's appointment as the Trust's chief executive in 1988 placed at its centre a vigorous, experienced educationist with definite ideas about improving urban education and making the process of learning more active.[4] The six curriculum development directors, dispersed around the country but networked to one another and to the Trust's small London office (as is appropriate for an IT-rich initiative), are sources of influence which feed into and from a large Curriculum Development Steering Committee composed of officers, sponsors and principals and so assist those (like Susan Fey) who see CTCs as a 'movement' rather than merely a collection of schools. Nevertheless, CTCs are independent schools. Trust staff have no right of entry; they need an invitation. Formally, and in this respect much more like representative bodies in the private sector than the LEAs of the past, they can work only by consent. As a project director put it approvingly, 'the Trust is there if we need advice, and it is an on-demand service rather than spoon-feeding us when they think we need something'. In our interviews with her, Susan Fey was adamant about not wanting to 'replicate a local authority', or to provide (for example) the kinds of consortium arrangements for buying educational supplies which would force the Trust to expand its administrative base rather than remaining 'very small, very flexible'. Her emphasis was on encouraging, by persuasion, the kinds of curriculum and pedagogic innovations we describe later in this chapter. In this respect, the Trust may resemble the LEA of the future in having to make its services worth asking for.

We recorded some feeling within CTCs that any money for curriculum development would be better dispersed than centralised. One principal asserted his dislike of any form of 'federation' and his determination not to acquire 'outside' advisers, though like Valerie Bragg at Kingshurst he was noted for maintaining strong defences even against visits from other

CTCs. Another principal found difficulty in defining the Trust's role beyond that of 'helping sponsors to get their act together to start a CTC', and criticised what he saw as its failure either to counter hostile press coverage effectively or resist attempts to evaluate CTCs prematurely. Another doubted the collective value of the curriculum development team, though he remained enthusiastic about 'a small number of institutions knit together by a common ethos'. As we illustrate when describing curriculum innovations post-16 which have benefited from some central impetus and co-ordination, the later CTCs seem markedly more co-operative in outlook than those in the first wave. But the predominant view is well summarised by another project director, who was convinced that CTCs worked

> better as a federation than as a sort of movement. I think each of the parts of the federation is entitled to go its own way and so contribute to the whole. . . . Now you can try to weld them together, and I'm sure there is a place for the Trust and the officers of the Trust, but if there is any attempt to hammer the pieces into a sort of mould, I think it would be resisted.

We turn now to the internal organisation of the 'pieces'.

As a prototype for breaking the LEA 'monopoly', the CTC programme was soon overtaken by the Reform Bill's provision for LEA schools to opt for direct government funding and for the 'independence' which that would bring. Although there was a well-publicised disagreement between Baker and Margaret Thatcher before the 1987 election about the likely and desirable scale of opting-out, any considerable movement of existing schools from LEA control would obviously create a far more substantial 'half-way house' between the public and private sectors than a small 'pilot network' could do. But CTCs went further in some of the directions recommended by the existing system's more radical critics.

The 'substantial contributions' of private money which proved so hard to secure were politically necessary as a justification for CTCs being 'owned (or leased) and run' by their promoters (DES 1986: 6). The securing of independence through the creation of a charitable trust has been the main mechanism advocated in New Right campaigning for self-governing schools, and was described by Kenneth Clarke in his 1991 North of England Education Conference as the 'natural organising model' for public provision in education and health. He went on to identify grant-maintained schools as the fullest exemplification of 'the initiative and creative thinking that I wish to see pervading the whole education service'. As registered independent schools, however, CTCs offer even more scope for 'initiative'.

From a hostile perspective, they have 'the capability of being run like purely commercial enterprises, with scant regard for educational and professional considerations' (NUT 1989). While they cannot be run for profit, and cannot charge fees, they undoubtedly offer their promoters unusual scope for shaping a school because sponsors have a built-in majority on governing bodies. They have to co-opt 'no fewer than four' other governors to represent teachers, other staff, parents and the wider community, but teachers themselves are excluded and parents have significantly less representation (from one to three members) than the five required for a maintained comprehensive school with a thousand pupils. That there is no LEA representative on the governing body of any CTC is a 'logical' consequence of the initiative's main political objective.[5] More generally, the composition of CTC governing bodies can be seen as marking the extent to which 'cosy' professional preserves have been broken into. At Kingshurst, for example, the first chairman was an executive from Turner and Newell, the vice-chair came from Hanson's, and three 'educationists' were outnumbered by seven other governors from business and industry. If the expertise and contacts available to schools from the composition of their governing bodies is a significant source of relative advantage and disadvantage, then CTCs may be particularly favoured. Thus one of its business members commented to us on the breadth of business experience represented on what Emmanuel CTC calls its 'board of directors', a board which includes the owners of two large north-east companies and executives from Laing's and Safeway.

Unless curbed by modern business belief in site management and executive responsibility, or of course by business pressures on the time of the 'directors', the possibility of something like 'company schools' emerging might seem considerable. Indeed, it was the gvernment's declared intention that the 'lead' sponsors, having made their contribution to the start-up costs of a new CTC, should continue to be a visible presence in its development so as to ensure that the school remained open to outside interests and responsive to the needs of local employers. There is also some resemblance to the tradition under which merchants, manufacturers and property speculators founded their own schools for meritorious children who could be suitably prepared for local employment. Certainly Sir Philip Harris, Harry Djanogly and Geoffrey Leigh take a close personal interest in the CTCs named after them, as do (for example) Peter Vardy in Emmanuel and Stanley Kalms in Dixon's. These are all individual entrepreneurs unlikely to be sleeping partners in any venture they supported. But executives from major national companies also tended at interview to emphasise the attractions of an educational initiative to which they were expected to contribute more than money and goodwill, and in which they could continue to feel actively involved. The possible threat to professional autonomy is perhaps most visible where a project director, seen as representing the lead sponsor, continues in office during a CTC's early development. Commenting on an inevitable tension once the principal had 'come on board', one project director remarked that it was then necessary to 'stand back and let the person have the chance to feel it's their show'. Another contrasted the lead sponsor's wish that 'his' CTC should be entirely businesslike in its running with the staff's wish to see 'the business approach kept at arm's length'. It was certainly made clear to us in several CTCs that the continuing presence of a project director after the school had opened was a cause of some awkwardness, but the undue interference from sponsors, trustees or boards of governors/ directors reported to us by individual teachers seemed to be the exception rather than the rule. We consider later indications of direct business influence on the curriculum of CTCs. At this point, our concern is with the 'businesslike' structure and style of management which CTCs might be expected to display.

In their registered independence, and in the 'proprietorial' rights of their sponsors and trustees, CTCs represent a 'half-way house' definitely inclined towards the private sector. In other respects, however, their management is claimed to be distinctive. Thus David Regan, Professor of Government at Nottingham University and a trustee and governor at Djanogly, describes that CTC as being unlike any school in either sector because it has a three-tier system of a board of trustees (the shareholders), a board of governors (the directors), and a consultative 'college council' to provide advice and ideas (Regan 1990: 28–9). That combination may be unique, though the notion of shareholders and directors is common to other CTCs and Dixon's (for example) has a council with pupil representatives, power to place items on its agenda as well as receive them from 'above', and the declared function of giving students 'experience of the democratic process'. There is an evident tendency to use business terminology and business titles. For example, it is common practice to refer to CTC principals (several of whom have management qualifications) as 'chief executives' even when the term is not formally used. Other management-style titles include the directors of finance and administration at Kingshurst and Macmillan, the directors of personnel and planning and of external services at Dixon's, the industrial and commercial liaison officer at Kingshurst, and the IT systems manager in several CTCs. It is doubtful, however, whether such terminology can be taken in itself as indicating distinctive forms of management.

In the first place, any claim to distinctiveness has to be examined in the context not only of grant-maintained schools but also of the simultaneous extension of site-management into LEAs themselves (Deem and Wilkins 1992). The autonomy given to CTCs to take their own decisions (within the limits set by their funding agreements and by the national curriculum) contrasts much less sharply with maintained secondary schools than appeared likely in 1986. It has been argued that heads of grant-maintained schools tend to exaggerate their new-found independence because they made that change before extensive LEA delegation of responsibility to schools had taken effect, and that the managerial demands now facing them are not necessarily more difficult or even very different (Halpin *et al.* 1991; 1992). It is clear, however, that grant-maintained schools, like CTCs, have more money to manage than comparable maintained schools, and many now employ business managers who are (as in CTCs) an integral part of the senior management team. Thus a much clearer division of labour between professional leadership and administrative infrastructure is not unique to CTCs. When the CTC Trust (1991a: 7) exemplifies the 'key staff' whom sponsors help to select as being 'the principal and the director of administration', it is assuming for that second role responsibilities extending far beyond those traditionally carried by the bursars of large private schools. In several CTCs, the original project directors have stayed on in this role, being appointed for qualifications and experience entirely outside education. For example, John Ramsden at Djanogly had been in business in Sheffield and Tim Willis at Macmillan the managing director of the local paper. Considerable use is made elsewhere of non-teachers in such specialist roles as IT systems manager or director of learning support services. Again, the practice is unusual but it can be found outside the CTC movement.

Another difficulty, encountered in most generalisations about CTCs, is their obstinate particularity. Taking examples from both ends of a managerial continuum, the ADT company appointed its own corporate affairs director as the formally designated 'chief executive' of its CTC on the grounds that a single principal would have an impossible task. The chief executive was there to ensure the smooth running of the CTC's administration, its relations with its sponsors and with external bodies. Alongside him was appointed a managing director (academic resources), responsible for the curriculum and, as senior professional, for the various managers of faculties. There the business model is evident, and the organisation highly unusual. In contrast, the CTC at Telford is called Thomas Telford School, thereby avoiding all three components of the normal title. Being a school, it has a 'headmaster'. Although he is a visiting lecturer at Manchester University's Business School, and although the school claims to benefit from consultants seconded from business and industry, the main management line is from head to seven deputies (effectively, the managers of broad curriculum areas) and then to curriculum team leaders. Other CTCs resemble Thomas Telford more than they resemble ADT in their top management. This is unsurprising when most CTCs have appointed as principals individuals already experienced in heading schools. They would presumably be unlikely to accept the ADT diagnosis of the role's unmanageability.

It is an article of faith among many advocates of deregulating educational supply that 'meaningful autonomy' requires freedom from external control, and that without such autonomy strong purposeful leadership is impossible. Having illustrated that conclusion from an analysis of US secondary schooling, John Chubb and Terry Moe (1992) pay particular attention to CTCs in their approving review of how the Reform Act is 'liberating' schools to make their own decisions. Yet there is also evidence in recent research on school improvement that self-managing schools are not necessarily less bureaucratic and more flexible in their internal structures (Ball and Bowe 1991; Louis and Miles 1992: 25–7), and that too much reliance is often placed on 'strong' leadership without due consideration of other factors making for successful innovation (Fullan 1991: 145–69; 1992: 82–96). Thus Louis and Miles's scepticism about 'the romance of leadership' in some accounts of organisational innovation is reinforced by doubts about whether there would be enough 'movers and shakers' to go around (1992: xii). Now CTCs have certainly recruited some charismatic 'movers' to their top posts. As we noted earlier, they have also recruited heads convinced that traditional forms of secondary schooling had failed and that CTCs had exceptional opportunities to 'break the mould'. In the rest of this chapter and the first part of the next, we consider some of the possibilities and limits of that freedom to experiment, and the uses to which it is being put. Before doing so, and with due regard for differences between CTCs, we make two generalisations about their management.

CTCs tend to have flatter hierarchies than conventional comprehensive schools, and they have conditions of service more closely akin to those in the private sector. A reduced number of managerial levels is partly a consequence of avoiding single-subject departments, partly reflects a commitment to sharing and rotating responsibilities rather than tying them to particular posts, and may represent some borrowing from 'post-Fordist' industrial organisation. It also contributes to the capacity of most CTCs, sometimes assisted by extra money from sponsors, to pay higher than average starting salaries across the board and then to give performance-related increments or 'bonuses' for teaching and other staff (including some principals). The coupling of such incentives with insecurity of tenure is described by Roger Dale (1990: 10) as 'the most thorough going attack yet on the role of the professional in education'. Such an attack seemed especially visible in the management refusal at Djanogly to negotiate salaries or conditions of service with any teacher association, and in the explicit no-strike clause in teachers' contracts which caused intense controversy at the time of its announcement.[6] More mundanely, the paying of above average salaries, which Dale might regard as compensation for loss of 'professional' rights, is also a contractual recognition of the longer teaching year and teaching day which CTCs require.

Both those aspects of reformed working practice were included by Kenneth Clarke among CTC innovations which should be 'of value and interest to all secondary schools' (CTC Trust 1991: 3). They were described by the DES in 1986 as the 'likely' solution to how to specialise in technology and science while retaining a broad, balanced curriculum. But the longer day is not made a contractual obligation by the DES, and there was scepticism about its benefits in several CTCs. Emmanuel's principal dismissed it as carrying a high risk of burning out teachers, and as depriving pupils of time they should be spending with their families. Another principal included among the 'crazy ideas' to which CTCs are subjected by their political promoters the notion that increasing the amount of time spent in classrooms brought a certain increase in learning. At least in theory, the longer school year provides time for staff training, staff work experience, and for the thematic and other curriculum experiments described later. Breaking up that year into five terms of equal length, a practice already adopted by four CTCs, is identified by one principal as exemplifying what can be done when schools are free to make their own decisions and encouraged to break with tradition. He describes it as a change which makes 'curriculum planning simpler and learning more effective' (Andrews 1991). We turn now to changes being made in the curriculum itself.

A DISTINCTIVE CURRICULUM 'MISSION'?

The autonomy which constituted the main political appeal of CTCs has been considerably constrained in relation to the curriculum. The constraints have produced some ambivalence towards CTCs among those wishing to see secondary schools freed to find whatever specialised niche in the market consumer demand will support. Thus, while welcoming CTCs as an 'anti-system reform', Chubb and Moe (1992: 28) regret the top-down approach to liberating the supply side and express a strong preference for allowing new schools to 'emerge of their own accord' rather than be prescribed by government.

In addition to highlighting in the naming of CTCs a curriculum specialisation which they would need to live up to, the DES (1986) warned prospective parents that the 'strong technical and practical element' would entail an 'unusual directiveness in what pupils could study in years 4 and 5'. It then gave four pages of a fifteen-page document to an 'illustrative curriculum' which it justified as embodying principles drawn from previous DES (though apparently not HMI) publications and from the 'curricular criteria for the extension of TVEI'. These guiding principles were then defined as breadth and balance, an emphasis on the practical applications of knowledge, and relevance to employment and the responsibilities of citizenship (DES 1986: 10).

The illustration of how these principles might be turned into practice was markedly less subject-centred than the government's consultative document on a national curriculum which followed in July 1987. Some subjects were subsumed within broad curriculum segments – for example, 'design and its realisation', 'business understanding and personal development', 'understanding industry', and a humanities group of subjects which 'might be taught separately or in various combinations' – and the whole model looked much less like the 'timetable of a country grammar school of the 1950s' which some critics claimed to recognise in the draft national curriculum (Haviland 1988: 13–69). Taken together, those segments representing the 'large technical and practical element' which the government was promising (design and technology, science, mathematics and 'understanding industry') were given a notional minimum allocation of around 55 per cent in Years 1–3 and 50 per cent in the largely 'directed, common core curriculum with limited optional choice' prescribed for the two years which followed.

That model was absorbed into a statutory national curriculum. As independent schools, it was initially thought that CTCs were either not bound by it or that they might be regarded en bloc as a 'special case' within the definition provided by section 16 of the Reform Act – namely, as schools freed from all or some statutory curriculum requirements to enable 'development work and experiments to be carried out'. In section 105, which dealt specifically but very briefly with CTCs, they are required to have 'a broad curriculum, with an emphasis . . . on science and technology or . . . on technology in its application to the performing and creative arts'. Although early official references were made to CTCs being bound by 'the substance of the national curriculum', the obligation to meet its requirements which is included in their funding agreements is as comprehensive as that placed on maintained schools. The effect can be illustrated by the fate of proposals for a suitably modern approach to the teaching of science and technology which the Organisation for Rehabilitation through Training (ORT) was invited in 1987 to provide for Kingshurst and Djanogly. Indeed, as late as January 1988, HMI were anticipating a significant role for ORT in designing the curriculum of other CTCs. But ORT's fundamental preference was for organising learning across subjects and around 'themes' and 'educational events'. While there are other reasons why their proposals were rejected, including what some working in CTCs regarded as insufficient knowledge of English educational practice, an obvious incompatibility with a subject-dominated national curriculum was prominent among them. A senior CTC teacher was later to describe to us, regretfully, how the national curriculum had strengthened the hand of those faculty heads who favoured a more traditional curriculum structure than CTC's innovative character had seemed to promise.

The constraints imposed by the national curriculum can be seen, however, as supporting Kenneth Baker's expressed dislike of premature specialisation, and his initial pledge that 'familiarity with IT and its applications' and 'a better understanding of an industrial society' would not be at the expense of 'English, humanities, modern languages, PE or the expressive arts' (cited in *New Scientist* 16 October 1986). Although the pledge was an immediate response to predictions that CTCs would become 'technological grammar schools' or 'inner-city forcing houses for science', the illustrative curriculum provided by the DES seems much less specialised than might have been expected of the 'sort of magnet school' which CTCs were being said to resemble. Nor does it seem especially 'modern', or to have any very obvious appeal to commerce and industry if employers' preference is taken to be a direct relationship to the 'world of work'. Indeed, Cyril Taylor (1987) was soon arguing for a stronger vocational bias, and for CTC sponsors to play a prominent part in curriculum development so as to promote that bias and to counter the traditional pressures favouring an 'academic' curriculum.

Any such bias, including the 'technical and practical' emphasis which the DES had promised, raised an obvious problem of how to make it compatible with breadth and balance. Kenneth Baker perceived a simple solution. As he explained to us:

> When I was at Education, I was told by experts that you could have any flexibility you want in the national curriculum if you had one more period a day. If you had one more 45-minute period a day in state schools, you could do the national curriculum – as it was legislated for, not as it's been changed to – with no trouble at all. Now what is happening in most CTCs is that they have that extra period, and some have two periods a day, and they can therefore do all sorts of extra flexible things.

Although that extra time is not taken by all CTCs, it is usually treated in Trust publications as a necessary condition for the 'value-added' curriculum being offered (CTC Trust 1991a: 9–10). Many of these publications are clearly intended to create and sustain a national identity for the 'movement'. Like the work of the TVEI Unit earlier, they are heavily imbued with curriculum evangelism and by a tendency to equate rhetoric with practice (Dale *et al.* 1990: 10). They also display an under-standable commitment to defining, justifying and illustrating, the 'particular CTC curriculum mission' of CTCs. In our analysis of that mission in practice, we concentrate on the three goals which Susan Fey (1991) identifies as constituting the distinctive CTC 'mission'. They are to increase the numbers of mathe-maticians, scientists and technologists through promoting a 'science and technology culture'; to develop a vocationally relevant curriculum through promoting a strong 'business and industry culture'; and to enhance the quality of learning through pervasive and effective use of IT. We then conclude our analysis of that mission with an area of curriculum innovation – the bridging of the 'academic'–'vocational' gulf post-16 – which is claimed from within the 'movement' as demonstrating an unusual capacity to challenge educational tradition.

A scientific and technological culture

The title which the CTC Trust gave to its 1991 progress report, 'A Good Education with Vocational Relevance', might be considered a distinct case of under-selling. There are connotations of the inferior status given to past departures from conventionally academic secondary education, 'vocational relevance' being seen as unfit for the future 'officer class'. In his introduction to that report, however, Sir Cyril Taylor presents CTCs 'as responding directly to the increasing preponderance of 'knowledge jobs' in the labour market, and so as preparing their students especially well for work in the high-tech areas of business and industry.

As we noted earlier, the 'technology' label raised familiar questions about whether priority was to be given to producing technicians or a technological elite. Even asking such questions, Denholm (1990a) argues, is to be 'lost in a 1930s time warp' because CTCs are not a revival of the old technical schools but a proper reflection of the dominance of 'scientific and technological modes of thinking' in the modern world. Similarly, Susan Fey (1991) places 'at the very heart of the educational environment' in CTCs a 'scientific and technological culture' rather than an inventory of useful skills, and a CTC head of 'science, mathematics and technology' drew a sharp contrast between ORT's interest in better-educated technicians with his own commitment to making scientific and technological modes of thinking and investigation central to the whole curriculum.

We recognise that counting timetabled hours is an inadequate measure of curriculum priority, especially in schools which make a particular display of 'extension' and 'enrichment' time. Nevertheless, we were surprised that the CTCs we visited were not giving greater prominence to such obvious sources of distinctiveness. A DES observer commented to us that CTCs had been expected and were trying to be innovative in too many directions at the same time, and that it would be wise to concentrate on enhancing students' achievements in science and technology because that would be distinction enough and would itself take 'all the time and energy available'. If he had been principal of Kingshurst, he argued, and so setting the pace, he would have worked to ensure that whatever else happened the teaching of science and technology was conspicuously good. Yet Walford and Miller (1991: 73) noted 'how little time' was given to those subjects, and the HMI report on Kingshurst (the first CTC to be given a full inspection) refers to a 'poor deployment' of resources in science and shortages of 'some mundane but necessary materials and equipment' in technology other than IT. Indeed, the 'craft and design aspects of technology' are picked out (along with modern languages) as having 'less than satisfactory standards' overall (DES 1991: 1). All CTCs have been visited less formally but often by HMI. Included in a general comment on the 'sound start' made by the seven CTCs operating in 1990–1 is the judgement that 'Standards in design and technology and in science, however, were variable and nowhere outstanding' (HMI 1992: 22). Although CTCs could argue that they have not yet had much time to become 'outstanding', it is still surprising that a more obvious priority has not been given to the two curriculum areas where (along with IT) conspicuous success will be expected. What adds to that surprise is that CTCs have generally been successful, as we showed earlier, in achieving intakes with roughly equal numbers of girls to schools explicitly oriented towards subjects in which they have been conspicuously under-represented. In that context, the promotion of a strong 'science and technology culture' may have quite particular benefits.

In our own visits to CTCs, we asked explicitly to be shown something of curriculum developments which the staff themselves regarded as innovative. In relation both to science, and to design and technology except for the example described below, there was no evidence of unusual teaching methods nor, to cite three of the indicators of curriculum priority which Fey (1991) suggests, of 'scientific and technological methodologies or contexts' being used in other curriculum areas, 'relevant applications from industry and commerce', or 'regular celebration of scientific and technological achievement'. Of course, most of the lessons we observed were at Key Stage 3 and such indicators might well be more apparent later. Certainly we saw a good deal of 'advanced' electronics and robotics equipment not yet in use. But while several CTCs workshops contained equipment larger and more sophisticated than is normally found in schools, we also recorded comments from some specialist teachers about the folly of trying to match industrial standards within the CTC rather than taking students out to real working environments.[7]

If science and technology seemed not to be getting a very much increased share of the timetable or permeating other subjects, neither did we see much evidence of a systematic weighting of 'enrichment' time or of the 'themes' and 'project weeks' which represent planned interruptions to the normal curriculum. We report one project, however, which illustrates both a 'practical' approach and a commitment to cross-curricular teaching. The reception desk at one CTC had been wrongly sited and was too small, and the improved version submitted by an outside firm had been rejected by the governors as too expensive. That real problem had been referred to a mixed-ability class of twenty-six Year 7 students who were given nine lessons in design and technology and in English to work in small groups on solving it. Their work included establishing what was needed by interviewing office staff, drawing and computer-modelling their designs, contacting suppliers, and presenting their proposals to teachers and governors. The successful team then took its design to a local manufacturer and had the final satisfaction of seeing it actually installed. The exercise seemed admirable, but we saw little else like it in other CTCs.

In contrast to their critical comments on design and technology at Kingshurst, HMI noted the 'confidence and success' with which its students used IT, and an enthusiasm for doing so which reflected the importance given to IT 'in many aspects of the college' (DES 1991: para 31). It has been a main educational objective of CTCs from the start to 'establish the value and effectiveness' of an especially IT-rich environment (DES 1986: 7). The extent of its transforming effects on teaching and learning is examined later, and we are concerned here with the special task, highlighted in many CTC publications, of preparing students for a world where computers, electronic mail and personal communication networks are so much part of everyday life that students should leave 'wholly confident in the use of IT in a range of applications from basic commercial uses to more specialized industrial and design functions of computer and multi-media technology' (CTC Trust 1991a: 9).

Preparing those students for IT-based 'knowledge jobs' is felt to carry a double obligation. First, IT facilities not only must be 'the very latest' educationally, but also must include equipment and systems currently used in the world outside education. The reality of that ambition is apparent where, as in the language learning systems at Djanogly and Leigh, the facilities are made available to local companies for their own staff training. Second, IT has to pervade the whole of the CTC's working life. A high density and quality of provision certainly makes that possible. A ratio of computers to students as high as 1: 3–4 should be compared with a normal ratio in maintained secondary schools of about 1:30, and with 1:18 achieved by the end of the IT-rich 'Education 2000' project (Fisher 1990). Dixon's for example, which one of its students told us offered 'all the things you need when you need them', already had over a hundred Olivettis, twenty RM-Nimbus, sixty Tannberg lap-top computers and a CD-ROM system. As the Trust's curriculum development director for IT has commented, an initial outlay of around £250,000 each has made CTCs 'interesting' to IT suppliers (Denholm 1991).

Such a level of provision may not be maintained as CTCs grow to their full size, and an IT co-ordinator was already conveying to us his alarm at DES failure to recognise either depreciation costs or the demands of updating hardware and software. Yet IT is certainly a very visible presence. Its visibility is enhanced by the wide distribution of machines around some CTC buildings; the physical centrality and multi-media aspect of the 'information' or 'resources' centres which replace 'libraries' in most CTCs; and by the use of electronic bulletin boards, CD-ROM, interactive video, and closed-circuit television to reinforce the high-tech aspects of the environment, There is also a strong emphasis on using IT routinely, and to be seen as doing so, for registering students, monitoring attendance, and recording academic performance (Lynch 1991). Such computerised management information is an important aspect of CTCs' commitment to be 'businesslike' in the several senses of that word.

A 'business and industry culture'

The CTC 'mission' is clearly seen as involving much more than specialised 'business education'. As Susan Fey (1991) puts it, CTCs should offer a thoroughly 'businesslike image' and a pervasive 'enterprise ethos'. It could hardly be otherwise when the paracurriculum was prescribed with unusual explicitness. CTCs were to develop the qualities of 'enterprise, self-reliance and responsibility' necessary for successful careers in an industrial culture (DES 1986: 4).

A businesslike image is certainly apparent. Kingshurst, planned by its principal to look very unlike an 'ordinary school', was described by one caustic journalist observer of its opening as a 'dream palace' for high-tech addicts, 'its cladding of burgundy and several shades of grey making it appear more like a corporate head office'. Although another observer from the same journal portrayed it more coolly as 'a cheap industrial building with burgundy trimmings', she too saw it as very unlike a school (*Times Educational Supplement* 30 September 1988, 1 June 1990). Telford's prospectus describes 'a spacious and light building which captures the atmosphere of the modern office', and quotes a pupil's (presumably appreciative) comment that being there is 'more like working in an office'. Dixon's architects intended their building to look more like a shopping mall than a school, and succeeded; however, the capacity of the main 'mall' to amplify noise elicited caustic comments from its principal. One of the present writers, visiting Emmanuel CTC the day after interviewing Lord Young at the Cable and Wireless head-quarters, found its reception hall more like that particular corporate head office in appearance and atmosphere than any comprehensive he had ever visited.

The private contributions to the capital funding of CTCs were intended not only to encourage a close alignment with business and industry, but also to give their sponsors (and other local employers) a direct voice in what is taught. It might therefore be expected that the curriculum is being shaped, quite openly, towards meeting those familiar complaints about the irrelevance of secondary schooling which we reviewed in earlier chapters. That shaping might be in relation to a general improvement in the educational standards, attitudes and therefore employability of youngsters from the inner-city, which was the main objective claimed by (for example) Harry Djanogly and Stanley Kalms, or to particular kinds of employment such as those in retailing which Emmanuel's sponsors emphasised. Sponsorship, and a consequent position as trustee and/or governor, provide individual entrepreneurs or company representatives with exceptional scope for active engagement with secondary schooling.

Such engagement is sometimes apparent. At Telford, for example, sponsors and other local firms contribute to the curriculum and its assessment by seconding specialist consultants, advising on quality assurance, providing work experience, and contributing financially to the funding of technician posts in IT, reprographics and systems design. In the ADT prospectus, sponsors are described as 'producing the curriculum', much of which is dependent on 'work-related activities in local firms'. The 'Business and Enterprise Pavilion' at Djanogly has within it a Centre for Industrial Studies, headed by a seconded Central Electricity Board executive, which is both a base for that part of the curriculum and a meeting place for local business people. Leigh's lead sponsor was described to us as wanting 'an industry-led curriculum with an international flavour', and that CTC's 'Business Centre' aims to take students through the entire manufacturing process from design and testing to marketing and to offer 'real business projects . . . in a fully equipped modern office'. Although the 'Bradford Business Partnership' seems to give much greater priority to cross-curricular problem-solving and collaborative groupwork than to inculcating economic awareness, it draws its problems from local businesses and emphasises their direct relevance to 'real work'.

These are obvious manifestations of a curriculum priority, as is the obligation to undertake industrial placements which is written into teachers' contracts at various CTCs. They are not unique to CTCs, of course, though they may become more conspicuous than in most maintained schools and they are certainly highly advertised. There is a more substantial example in the emphasis on business needs in the foreign language teaching at Leigh and Macmillan, an emphasis which led to the inclusion of 'languages for commerce and industry' among the six areas to be supported by the curriculum development unit created in 1989. The Trust's curriculum development director for modern foreign languages had worked intensively on 'the foreign language challenge facing British industry' before his appointment, and the Trust circulated his various papers on that challenge and on 'the vocational relevance of linguistic proficiency'. He himself writes enthusiastically about how foreign language teaching has flourished 'within the overtly high status vocational learning environment of the CTCs' (Hagen 1992).

In their full report on Kingshurst, HMI comment on students' 'unusually good understanding of economic issues and business organisation'. That reference was not to the BTEC courses which that first CTC had already established, but to the curriculum for Years 7–9. In HMI's view, few pupils in other secondary schools would be able at that stage 'to discuss issues such as the

European market and its consequences for British firms' (DES 1991: para 34). There is no indication, however, as to how that remarkable understanding had been achieved and whether it was an outcome of unusually effective direct teaching or of instruction permeating other areas of the curriculum. In our own classroom observations we recorded few examples of such permeation, apart from an English lesson focused entirely on what should be found out about a firm before being interviewed for a job there – 'its market share, who its suppliers are, and so on' – and then about how a firm might weigh the advantages and disadvantages of running its own transportation system against using a specialist company. The homework was to list examples of unreliable products which students had recently encountered and then note whether or not these were British-made! We have no way of knowing how typical was such overt vocationalising of a subject, or of the assembly address given live on closed-circuit television in which the principal of the same CTC built with calm dexterity two 'houses' of cards and then successfully laid other cards across the gap between them to illustrate his message about building bridges between industry and the [—— CTC] experience'.

A shift from teaching to learning?

The development of 'new and improved approaches to teaching and learning' is identified by HMI as an obligation placed on CTCs, and so as a criterion against which they had observed practice at Kingshurst (DES 1991: para 1). It is an obligation included in CTCs' initial remit, which refers to the importance of 'doing and understanding as well as knowing' and so implies that conventional secondary education is overweighted with 'academic' information and with outmoded methods of trans-mitting it. It is also an obligation given considerable prominence in Trust and CTC publications, which display a determination to work across conventional curriculum boundaries, and a wish to encourage more active, investigative and collaborative styles of learning. There is frequent reference to developing skills of finding and using information so that students can work independently, and teachers can concentrate on how best to organise the conditions for effective learning rather than controlling its pace from the front of the class. It was the exceptional opportunity to 'trial and evaluate new modes of learning' which Susan Fey identified as having been her main reason for accepting her post at the CTC Trust (*Guardian* 12 September 1989), and she described in our first interview with her a 'road to Damascus' experience when a group of adult students had complained that she was intervening too persistently in their learning group and should 'go away until needed'. That notion of shifting the emphasis from teaching to learning recurred in many of our interviews with CTC staff, as did a confidence that the didacticism which they believed had plagued secondary education could at last be successfully challenged in the 'mould-breaking' environment which CTCs are believed to offer.

The conditions for doing so include, in the design of the newly built CTCs, the central position and high visibility of 'Information' or 'Resources' centres, and an unusually generous provision of 'common use' space – that is, space not marked out into classrooms but available for activities which spill out from their initial classroom setting. Thus when the prospectus for Bacon's CTC (for example) refers to a 'building designed for learning', it is a distinctively less teacher-centred approach to learning which is being presented: central to that distinctiveness are the high density and the variety of IT provision. Alongside the direct vocational value of developing familiarity and facility with modern technology is the intention that it should 'empower' students by giving them means of finding, sifting and presenting information which are not dependent on the teacher's media-tion. It is in this aspect of their work that CTCs claim to be at the 'leading edge of change' and aspire to a 'genuine beacon effect' by giving priority to developments which may be replic-able in reasonable time in maintained schools (Denholm 1990b).

Given the very short time that CTCs themselves have been operating, and the likely lag between good intentions and practice, it would be premature to 'test' the programme's success by the extent of pedagogic innovations so far. Yet while we sometimes shadowed individual students through a day's time-table, we also made explicit in most visits our particular interest in seeing teaching which the CTC itself regarded as promisingly different. Much of what we observed was therefore intended not to be typical.

Our main conclusion from observation in forty lessons in six

CTCs is that the teaching very rarely departed from the well-grooved channels of teacher-centred interaction. We certainly saw in some CTCs unusually extensive use of IT facilities during breaks in the timetable, much of it technological games-playing but some arising from the formal curriculum. Unsupervised users of IT were also observed in 'information centres' or other public areas, engaged in tasks relating to their lessons. But we recorded few instances of computers being used during lessons not timetabled as IT except for several foreign language classes. The examples which follow fairly represent the lessons we saw in being skewed more to traditional than innovative methods.

In a Year 8 humanities lesson, pupils were seated at rows of desks tracing a diagram on soil erosion. Several comments to the teacher that the task was boring elicited as explanation that in working life they would face boring tasks much of the time. One boy suggested that the topic belonged to science not geography, and was told that subject boundaries are not important in humanities. A thoroughly didactic lesson on Henry VIII's achievements included written work for which the answers were ready-made in the textbook. An English class designing a dog-walking machine used no IT, did no work as groups, and left the room 'girls first . . . now the lads'. A German lesson would have pleased advocates of formal grammar ('add the accusative endings'), but included no use of the overhead projector, large video or tutordek and the students reported no familiarity with any of that equipment. Students in a science class talked fluently about their self-assessment, in which they have to identify and report what they have enjoyed, found difficult, and defined as their next learning priorities. Several had forgotten their targets; one had 'enjoyed air, got on well with life, and struggled with materials'. In a timetabled IT lesson, partly given over to instructions on the students' individual 'IT skills log', the Year 7 class were invited to compare spread sheets and data bases for the kinds of questions they could be 'asked', and then to work on how dates of birth should be recorded for the most convenient sorting. The carefully planned lesson was carried through in a benign schoolmasterly style, 'upgraded' by some challenging questions which included why the computer 'is confused when it's expecting a number and gets an alpha numeric'. A Year 8 drama lesson began with the teacher's commendation for previous class work 'on sub-text which I never thought you'd do so well'. Role-playing scenes were carried through with panache, especially by the girl who proposed marriage to a briefly overwhelmed boy, and there was a high level of participation in the discussions which followed them. A Year 7 design and technology class were preparing to present to the CTC's chair of governors their various designs for improving the open area outside their room. They were using, in small teams, a wide range of design, IT and presentational skills on a real problem, and the teacher (who had been co-leader of the 'reception desk' project referred to earlier) was unobtrusively but imaginatively supportive. The entire Year 7 had recently spent a day at the country estate belonging to one of the CTC's sponsors, engaged on team tasks which included an Arthurian game for which teachers and parents had acted at different sites parts of narrative puzzle which had to be solved. The follow-up tutorial focused on how well the various teams had performed, the tutor being an IT technician and not a qualified teacher.

Neither individual lessons nor the range of approaches is surprising. Nor is the apparent absence of a concerted, systematic 'shift from teaching to learning'. Although most CTCs are able to recruit an entire teaching staff, in theory against criteria derived from a particular curriculum mission, the attractiveness evident in a high ratio of applicants to jobs reflects their novelty and apparently high level of resourcing as well as what may be perceived as unusual scope for pedagogic experiment. One principal told us how he asked all his staff to question seriously how they've taught before, and to see themselves in their new setting as directors of studies and not providers of packaged knowledge. Then he added – 'But it's going to take time, and we've recruited some ordinary traditional teachers'. At Haberdashers', Bacon's and Leigh, many teachers have been inherited from the secondary schools which those CTCs replaced. There the situation is closer to the 'Education 2000' project where an IT-based 'shift from teaching to learning' was attempted in already existing schools. An independent evaluation of that project noted how teachers tended to see it more as an IT initiative than as a pedagogic experiment, and to use the rapidly extended IT provision more to support existing styles of teaching than to transform them (Ouston 1990). In short, IT was used to give old didacticism new apparel rather than to transform it. As Janet Ouston comments, the assumption that it could do otherwise ignores those powerful constraints in favour of teachers' close control of the knowledge being transmitted which classroom research has documented. Thus while a main objective of 'E2K' was to turn teachers 'from instructors to facilitators', from being the main source of information to what CTCs tend to term 'managers of the learning environment', there was little evidence of the deeper changes in perception and practice necessary to bring that about.

Much of the CTC rhetoric about pedagogic innovation is more about prospect than practice, and is often recognised as being so. We can illustrate this from a CTC where particular emphasis is given to the nature and quality of its IT provision. The head of information services, described by a senior colleague as having the clearest view of the CTC's overall educational strategy, had a strong background in computing but none in teaching. His staff of nine, paid on the same salary scale as teachers, provide services of high technical quality but he spoke eloquently of the effort needed to make them an integral part of teaching rather than a sophisticated but separate addition. In his view, many teachers feared 'losing control over their bits of knowledge and having their closed doors opened'. One of his fellow 'senior managers' commented on the continuing need to move 'from a computer studies to an IT mentality', and a vice-principal remarked that because teachers were accustomed to professional hierarchy, territory and privacy, it was considerably innovative to challenge all three simultaneously. The extent of that challenge is recognised, as it was in 'Education 2000', in a strong emphasis on staff development and by some individual CTCs (Gillman 1990/1).

We turn finally to an area of their work in which CTCs not only claim an exceptional capacity to challenge tradition but also are claiming significant achievements already.

Breaking with tradition in post-16 provision

There are considerable structural differences between CTCs at the post-16 stage. Thus Kingshurst recruits directly a large post-16 entry and Djanogly a small, multi-ethnic and relatively specialised one; Macmillan and Emmanuel intend to 'grow their own', partly so as not to exacerbate already hostile relationships with LEAs and neighbouring schools by directly threatening the viability of neighbouring provision; Leigh is seeking to build up post-16 work in a previously low-status school, and Harris to create it in what had been an 11–16 school. But this organisational diversity is seen within the movement as unimportant compared with the fact that CTCs have 'the high status and industrial backing to break the mould of academic 16+' (Taylor 1990: 24). As Susan Fey (1989) puts it, the very term sixth form 'carries traditional connotations which are not in line with the CTC vision'. It is a 'vision' or 'mission' in which 'raising the status of vocational qualifications and integrating business culture into the curriculum are central themes' (Jones 1992: 4).

They are themes followed for a highly ambitious purpose. Among the main objectives set for CTCs in 1986, and accepted as a measurable indicator of their performance, is to raise staying-on rates in urban areas where the waste of talent is conspicuous. It is a target set in the context of persistently unfavourable national comparisons, both of general participation rates in post-16 education and training and of the proportion of school-leavers with credible qualifications in science and technology (Fey 1989; Finegold *et al.* 1990; Smithers and Robinson 1991). By setting their own intended staying-on rate at 60–70 per cent, CTCs are accepting a target more readily associated with grammar schools or suburban comprehensives than with the kinds of catchment areas and intakes which CTCs have been prescribed. Though parental commitment to seven years of full-time education remains among the government's imposed entry criteria, there is no way of guaranteeing it at the point of application and no way of enforcing it if pupil or parental ambitions falter. It is therefore clear that CTCs must offer a range of curriculum choices at sixteen very different from the academic studies which have dominated the English sixth form.

In doing so, they see themselves as uniquely placed to challenge the entrenched narrowness of the 'academic' route, its sharp separation from the 'vocational' route, and above all the validity of making that distinction at all. Introducing a recent Trust report on 'bridging the divide', the deputy chief executive of the National Council for Vocational Qualifications describes CTCs as a 'fertile ground for experimentation' because of their close links with business and industry, responsiveness to local employment needs, 'imaginative use of work experience' and other ways of 'blurring the distinction between learning and work' (Gilbert Jessup, in Jones 1992). CTC representatives would add to those 'fertile' conditions an emphasis on the application of knowledge, and (of special significance in a country where only 13 per cent of those staying on after 16 take science and mathematics) an insistence that those subjects are the foundation for practical studies like engineering and not merely subjects for the 'academic'.

It is not surprising then that CTCs have been involved in some way in all recent reforms in post-16 provision – the development of a unit-based curriculum, credit transfer and the accrediting of prior learning, records of achievement, core skills, total quality management, BTEC and the combining of different qualifications within the NCVQ (National Council for Vocational Qualifications) framework (Jones 1990; 1992). Several of these developments merit highlighting. Kingshurst made an early decision not to offer A-levels, but to provide instead a choice between the International Baccalaureate and BTEC. Since the decision coincided with the then Prime Minister's strenuous defence of A-level, it is not surprising that DES officials gave anxious warnings against risking the reputation of a new school still establishing itself. Susan Fey herself noted that since it was also an ambition of CTCs to raise entry levels to higher education, 'we would be foolish to be so keen on breaking moulds that we threw A-levels out of the window' (Fey 1989: para 7.3). But even the initial DES brochure had given a mildly encouraging nod towards a 'mixed economy' at what it continued to call 'the sixth form stage', and this is manifestly what CTCs provide. Thus Kingshurst's 'unusual if not unique range of post-16 courses' (DES 1991: para 13) included (like other CTCs) a common core of general and 'transferable' skills. It also offered a 'Kingshurst Diploma' in which credit was given for achievements in science, mathematics, business awareness, IT, a foreign language, and 'social service, responsibility and leadership'. More generally and influentially, BTEC National Diplomas had been excluded from schools by administrative barriers designed to preserve them within the territory of Further Education. CTCs used their independence to ignore that restriction, after which the secretary of state could hardly deny to maintained schools what CTCs were already providing. The dismantling of a barrier which she attributed to institutionalised inertia was described to us by Susan Fey as an early, tangible example of a pilot network 'licensed' to take risks using that 'license' for the benefit of the system at large. Finally, the Technological Baccalaureate being developed by four CTCs, in co-operation with City and Guilds and the CTC Trust, is intended to be an ambitious attempt to go beyond merely 'bridging' the academic–vocational divide. It seeks to incorporate both in a single qualification achieved through various units and modes of study developing from a common core (CTC Trust 1991b). Intended to increase participation rates post-16 by confronting the 'English' assumption that vocational education is for those not capable of academic study, it also reflects an assumption that any 'subject can be approached from academic, vocational, artistic or employment related perspectives, and that the acquisition of knowledge should be explicitly related to learning 'how to do things as well as know about them' (Jones 1992: 20).

However, despite their promise, these post-16 initiatives are still in an embryonic phase of development, and it has yet to be seen whether the claims made for them in the promotional rhetoric of CTC Trust publications will actually be borne out in practice.

A NEW KIND OF SCHOOL?

'The school of tomorrow for the children of today' is the marketing slogan of Emmanuel CTC, and exemplifies that self-presentation as 'schools of the future' which we illustrated earlier. The modernity of CTCs is most visible in the design of the buildings and in the ubiquity of computers and other new technology. It may become more significant, and the evidence is as yet insufficient, in commitment to a new style of learning and especially in what has been called the 'new vocationalism'. It is under that heading that the apparent 'progressivism' of CTCs' emphasis on (for example) more practical, investigative and collaborative forms of learning can be reconciled with the expectation that they should provide a form of secondary education directly relevant to the personnel requirements and the culture of modern industry. For an approach to the curriculum and to its delivery which has at least a superficial resemblance to Lawrence Stenhouse's advocacy of 'mastery of seeking' over 'mastery of knowing' can also be given a quite different justification as a response to the differently skilled workforce which a modern economy demands (Edwards 1992).

That reconciliation is not easy, however, and we share Stephen Ball's view that CTCs represent 'a terrain of struggle between two conceptions of knowledge' (Ball 1990: 118). For while a central tenet of the new vocationalism is that any subject may be approached 'academically' or 'practically', and that the division of the 'academic' from the 'vocational' is therefore invalid, CTCs are still vulnerable to being rejected by what Ball calls the 'cultural restorationists' because they are seen as departing too radically from traditional subjects authoritatively taught. Continuing his earlier criticism of 'policies which are the educational equivalent of the tower blocks and town centre developments of the 1960s' in their obsession with utility (O'Hear 1987: 102), Anthony O'Hear brings together several elitist strands in a single rebuke by portraying CTCs as liable to produce technology-obsessed (and presumably uncultured) professionals, or technicians equipped with 'modern' skills who will merely be 'the Bob Cratchits of the future . . . tied to their computer screens for the rest of their lives without even the Victorian clerk's pride in his handwriting' (cited in Regan 1990: 36).

CTCs might reply in their defence that their adherence to the 'new vocationalism', especially as a means of increasing participation rates post-16 by challenging the traditional superiority of 'academic' studies, is both a response to economic imperatives and a matter of educational conviction. It is less clear that they are also responding to specific consumer demand. In the opening chapters, we referred to the long tradition in Britain of undervaluing technical and vocational education, and to the ambivalence of free market advocates like Stuart Sexton towards such a conspicuous government intervention in educational provision as the CTC programme represented. The targeting of substantial resources and considerable publicity on a few schools might of course be defended as helping to create a demand, and we have recorded some very positive consumer responses to the 'very latest' facilities which CTCs have so vigorously advertised. But we also noted a considerable regard for less modern characteristics when parents and children were making their choice of school.

Our interviews also included questions about how CTCs were perceived some time after entry. The level of expressed satisfaction was high, though ironically and especially at Harris there were complaints at a lack of computers and at a failure to use them widely in the curriculum. But what Harris parents emphasised was more often the orderliness of the school and the happiness of their children than those intended innovations in curriculum or teaching which we have described. Mrs Gambon was typical of many parents in liking 'the discipline and the fact that there's a lot of it'. Her daughter had 'a datalog so I know all I need to know – if there's a problem, the tutor will write it in', and she was confident that 'this wandering around the street and smoking' was not going to happen at the CTC. We even gathered some comments that Harris was not 'old fashioned' enough, being insufficiently 'hot on grammar and correcting spelling mistakes'.

Students too commented on a shortage of computers, which may well have been a temporary problem of transition from maintained comprehensive to the provision expected of a CTC. There were also complaints at the amount of homework and the length of the school day. But their largely positive views resembled, both in level of approval and in what was appreciated, the broadly pro-school attitudes recorded by Walford and Miller (1991) at Kingshurst and by ourselves for a much larger sample of pupils in independent and maintained schools (Edwards *et al.* 1989). If there was less recognition that these were 'schools with a difference' than the schools themselves might have hoped for, there were few doubts that they were getting a 'good' education. When Emmanuel CTC was given its first termly report by a local paper, the eulogy was headed 'Experimental college makes the grade with old values' and gave prominence to a parent's view that 'it's a return to old-fashioned teaching standards, school is the way it was when we were young and the children love it' (*Evening Chronicle* 19 December 1990). Though Emmanuel is exceptional among CTCs in its overtly evangelical origins and the commitment of its sponsors to restoring 'old values', that combination of tradition and 'experimentation' is apparent though less obvious in other CTCs. It raises questions about the nature of the changes they are making, and about their generalisability to the system at large.

Chapter 6

Disturbing the system?

From the outset, city technology colleges were presented as a source of disturbance in the system – one of those necessary 'points of creative energy' to which Kenneth Baker has referred. They would provide salutary competition for 'failing' comprehensives in urban areas where education was most in need of improvement, and demonstrate what could be achieved by schools freed from LEA control.

Having explored directions in which CTCs may be becoming especially innovative, we now examine these intended systemic effects. We begin with the function most often highlighted within the CTC 'movement', that of providing 'beacons of excellence'. We then examine the direct impact of some CTCs on the network of secondary schools into which they have been intruded, and on individual schools within that network. Finally, we discuss attempts to adapt the original CTC model in voluntary-aided and grant-maintained guise and the key role allotted to CTCs in the 1992 White Paper's proposals for diversifying educational provision (DFE 1992).

THE BEACON EFFECT

In defending his 'pilot network', Kenneth Baker promised that CTCs would be not only 'islands of excellence' in an otherwise failing system, but also 'lights for others to follow'.[1] The enthusiasm with which that wider obligation has been accepted within the CTC 'movement' reflects the discomfort noted earlier about the initiative's political objectives, and a consequent marked preference for being seen educationally as breaking the mould in a new setting where risks couldd be taken because traditions were not set. But there are also tactical reasons why CTCs' piloting function has been emphasised so strongly. First, it provides protection against jibes at the continuing failure to reach the target of twenty CTCs of the original model. If they are beacons, it can be argued, then quality matters more than number. Second, it provides a defence against criticism that too much money and attention are being concentrated on a favoured few, and aligns the initiative more clearly with the government's broader preference for targeting within its inner-city interventions. Replying to Professor Ted Wragg's attack on CTCs as an unnecessary extravagence, Sir Cyril Taylor emphasised the importance of their 'beacon or lighthouse effect' before arguing that if they provided a demonstrably high-quality 'relevant education for a wide range of ability with the same recurrent funding as maintained schools', then even their critics might overcome their distaste (*Times Educational Supplement* 10 March 1989).

For that counter-argument to be persuasive, however, certain conditions need to be met. CTCs have to be sufficiently different to justify special status and funding, and to demonstrate how uncommon secondary schools can find a niche and prosper. Yet they must not be too eccentric to be inimitable. Furthermore, they must not be so favoured, either in funding or in the selectiveness of their intakes, that any achievements can be explained away as being the outcome of special circumstances and so irrelevant to the development of 'normal' schools. We now consider how far those conditions are being met.

Complaints that CTCs are unfairly positioned to break new ground have been accompanied from the start by claims that they are doing nothing useful which cannot be matched in maintained schools. The sorts of problems described in chapter 3 led to opportunism about sites, and the creation of a supposed 'new choice of school' in areas where there was no evidence that it was needed or even that the education system was 'under most pressure'. Thus Bob Dunn's pleasure that several technical secondary schools had survived in his constituency did not prompt him to ask why a CTC was also needed in Dartford. This irony was again evident in Croydon, where one of the nearest competitors to Harris CTC was another of the few remaining technical high schools in Britain. Indeed, the headteacher of Stanley Technical High School for Boys explained to us that 'in a funny sort of way this school could be considered the 1907 version of a CTC'. It was in 1907 that W.S. Stanley, a local engineer concerned about his inability to recruit apprentices, had set up a school in his garden and so anticipated Cyril Taylor's (1987) argument that CTCs could help to remedy skills shortages by teaching 'the high quality technical courses relevant to the needs of local employers'. Stanley's creation developed with the help of his company from a trade school into a technical school and then a technical grammar school and it is now a voluntary aided comprehensive school. It has foundation governors from the company founded by Stanley and a chair of governors who is also the managing director of that company. Links with the company are also maintained through visits, though the company's once substantial direct financial contribution has dropped to a few hundred pounds a year – possibly a sign of the future facing CTCs once their original sponsors have lost interest, lost money, or for other reasons withdrawn support.

Although Stanley Tech is now a comprehensive school, teaching the national curriculum, it is still perceived by parents as having a technical bias and it was the first school in Croydon to offer computer studies. Regarded as being successful, and therefore oversubscribed, its main disadvantage has been a lack of recent investment. That condition provoked the governors to suggest in writing to Kenneth Baker that the money being invested in CTCs might be better used to upgrade existing schools of proven worth. Ironically, in view of what was to happen at Sylvan, they were told that CTCs had to be started from scratch. Yet another irony, given the siting of a dyslexia unit at Harris, is that Stanley has a particularly good reputation for teaching dyslexic children and is recommended to parents by the Dyslexia Association. If CTCs were intended to prefigure a wholesale move to specialisation and diversity in secondary education, then the locating of Harris CTC just down the road from Stanley Technical High seems a curious policy decision. While it might have made sense to provide parallel provision for girls in the area, 'there's very little that a CTC does that we don't do', as the head of Stanley put it.

Similarly, Solihull LEA had been in the first wave of TVEI pilot schemes, and three of the schools in Kingshurst's catchment area were involved in that initiative. Did such pioneering constitute a case for or against siting the first CTC in Solihull? The case has been argued both ways. Walford and Miller (1991: 30–2) describe one of those schools (Park School) as a conspicuous example of CTC characteristics being displayed in advance of the new model, with its extensive IT provision, strong links with local industry, and vocational provision post-16. Its head was also an energetic publicist of such innovations (Slater 1987; 1988). However, Edward Simpson, former DES deputy-secretary and adviser to Stanley Kalms (Dixon's) on his prolonged search for a suitable CTC site in the north of England, was reported as seeing particularly good opportunities in Bradford because the city's schools had been at the forefront of TVEI and so 'knew about' educational innovation (*Times Educational Supplement* 11 November 1988). Yet, it could have been argued with equal or greater force that Bradford was therefore less in need of whatever stimulus a CTC might provide than were less innovative LEAs.

Furthermore, those 'value added elements' in the CTC curriculum which we described in chapter 5 would be claimed as normal practice by many comprehensive schools, especially where they had been early participants in TVEI. Our interviews in comprehensive schools within CTC catchment areas often elicited firm claims to being capable of matching anything the CTC was doing given comparable resources. On their side, CTC staff were often cautious themselves in the claims they made. Replying to our usual question about whether the innovations being described had needed a CTC setting, one principal replied:

> To have got them off the ground in the way that we have, with the speed that we have, with the commitment to extending them, yes I think we probably did. But it's not to say that other schools can't do them, or that other schools aren't doing them already. . . . I'm never going to say that we are the only people doing something, and I don't think we ever will be. But I do think we have an opportunity to do them in a particular way.

Such caution often reflected a wish not to further antagonise heads of local schools and others threatened by the new venture. In addition, CTCs have recruited their heads mainly from urban comprehensives, and their perceived suitability for the post has often included an impressive record of successful innovation within the maintained sector. For example, Matt Andrews (Djanogly) was described by his project director as having 'developed what was virtually a miniature industrial estate' at his previous school, and then used it as a setting for technology and other projects. Gareth Newman at Corby had been a highly effective fund-raiser and promoter of links with industry in his previous comprehensive headships, and an advocate of flexible learning methods supported by modern technology. Thomas Telford's head described at interview not only curriculum innovations at his previous Wolverhampton comprehensive (a TVEI school) which closely resembled CTC aspirations, but also unusually successful links with local industry. Dixon's principal came from the headship of one of the few new maintained secondary schools built during the 1980s, and its prospectus bore a striking resemblance to the CTCs' in appearance and in emphasising the 'latest' in new technology and 'practical work in a problem-solving context'. Our question to principals about what they felt able to do which had been out of reach in their previous school gained force from knowing something of their previous record of innovation in LEA settings supposedly hostile to change.

Commentators on the programme as a whole have given very different answers when that question is put in general form. To critics, the key is money. Responding to Cyril Taylor's recent claims about the 'beacon or lighthouse effect' of CTCs, the president-elect of the Secondary Heads Association asked whether maintained secondary schools would have the same capital outlay; if not, then Taylor 'is employed to seek advantage for a privileged few' (*Times Educational Supplement* 10 March and 17 March 1989). Versions of that view underlie most of the fiercest attacks on the programme. Its supporters have tended to argue that the key to its success 'is not money, but autonomy and ideas', the essential condition being dynamic leadership and the autonomy which makes such leadership possible (Chubb and Moe 1992: 26, 28). We take up these explanations in turn, having already dealt in detail in chapter 4 with the less than obvious ways in which CTCs may be advantaged by their intakes.

Charges of unfair funding have been levelled at the initiative from its start. They include the capital investment needed to provide the visibly modern 'environment for learning' displayed by those CTCs which have been newly built or largely rebuilt, a modernity the more striking because there are so few other new schools with which to compare them. In a rare opportunity for comparison, Colin Standfield Smith won the RIBA's Royal Gold Medal in 1991 for having designed for Hampshire LEA a 'superb' new secondary school (Crestwood) which 'revolutionised the idea of the school' by moving away from the system-build, standardised pattern to a covered street/arcade design which – like Dixon's 'shopping mall' design – deinstitutionalised the setting (Rogers 1991). More generally, the innovative appearance of CTCs owes more to their being new than to exceptional capital expenditure. But while the price per square foot might be calculated as though for a maintained school of similar intake, CTCs have the distinct advantage of having been designed for their specialised character – in particular, for unusually extensive and diffused IT systems.

In its calculating of CTCs' recurrent expenditure, as we showed in chapter 3, the DES was perceived by CTCs themselves as having seriously underestimated their special costs. The problems referred to most often in interviews were a failure (more accurately, the Treasury's failure) to recognise the exceptional depreciation and running costs arising from unusually high levels of IT provision, and the heavy recurring costs of a significantly longer working year. That first 'blindspot' has apparently infuriated trustees and governors who fail, from their business experience, to understand it. As a Trust representative explained:

> Now if you're running something efficiently, you cost-in depreciation do you not? Depreciation doesn't exist in the Treasury. It is not a Treasury concept. We are not allowed to put depreciation in our budgets.

There was also a strong feeling that staff were sustaining unusual working conditions through their own unpaid efforts. After commenting that the DES had recognised 'the *danger* of producing better education with better money', a project director went on to estimate that his CTC needed to raise around £100,000 a year because

> the DES has chosen to ignore the financial implications of a 25 per cent longer teaching year. You can get people to work

that much harder in the first flush of enthusiasm for a new venture, but not when things have settled down. Initially —— [a DES official] spoke about salaries taking into account the extra hours worked, but that idea soon disappeared down a crack in the floorboards. So if the DES don't produce better money, we're going to end up with perhaps a marginally better comprehensive school, and the CTC movement will fail.

Whatever the inclination to give its pilot programme a flying start, the government has been inhibited by its belief in the programme's 'beacon' effect. Thus a DES window display (February 1990) told passers-by that, although CTCs were specially equipped for their specialised curriculum, this was 'to no higher level than can be attained by any state school within its existing budget' and claimed that it was because they were operating in comparable conditions that they could act 'to generally raise the level of accommodation, education and expectations across secondary schools'. Figures provided by the Schools Minister (Tim Eggar) were intended to support that claim to comparability, and are given in Table 6.1.

Table 6.1 Recurrent funding of CTCs for the school year 1991–2

CTC	Unit costs per pupil[a] (£)	Unit costs per pupil at full capacity[a] (£)	Unit costs per secondary pupil in local LEA[b]	(£)
Kingshurst	3,036	2,459	Solihull	1,914
			Birmingham	2,052
Macmillan	3,830	2,450	Cleveland	2,034
Djanogly	3,940	2,430	Nottinghamshire	2,168
Dixon's	6,527	2,540	Bradford	1,687
Harris	3,899	2,736	Croydon	2,015
Leigh	3,173	2,448	Kent	1,749
Emmanuel	7,206	2,430	Gateshead	2,031
			Newcastle	1,925

Notes: [a] Unit costs are inevitably high in the start-up period; the second column gives the estimated unit costs, at constant 1991–2 prices, when each CTC is operating at full capacity.
(Taken from a parliamentary written answer to Joan Ruddock, MP, 19 July 1991)
[b] The LEA figures are taken from the Chartered Institute of Public Finance Accountants (CIPFA) (1992) *Education Statistics 1990–91 Actuals*, London: CIPFA, pp. 32–3 and 49–51

As in all calculations of comparability, both statistics and the conclusions drawn from them vary with the perspective of the commentator. Critics of CTCs have certainly felt able to construct and maintain the appearance of favourable treatment. One critic, particularly partial because of his enthusiasm for the alternative, claims that 'Education 2000' represents 'a twenty-fold increase in efficiency over the politicised CTCs' as a way of funding curriculum and pedagogical change because its total private sponsorship of £1.5 million spread over four years (which meant no more than £105 a year extra spending on the 3,500 pupils affected, an addition of only 6.25 per cent on the LEA's per capita spending) meant that the money sunk into CTCs could have funded fifty more projects of the Letchworth kind (Fisher 1990: 31–2). Hertfordshire's average per-pupil grant (APG) was then significantly below the figures for CTCs, but it was not of course serving a 'comparable' area. A more realistic comparison is between the £1.53 million spent by Croydon on the 780 pupils in Sylvan School's last year, and the £2.97 million recurrent grant provided by the DES for Harris CTC in its first year when it had 757 pupils (*Guardian* 12 July 1991). On the crudest of comparisons, that gives APG figures of £1,961 and £3,923 respectively. In addition, Harris received the first instalment of a four-year grant of £281,000 for special provision in IT and technology. Its extra funding would seem hard to justify as being necessary to transform an already existing school. Similarly, while the justification for initial per capita funding well above the longer-term projected level and above that of other local schools is obvious in the case of schools building up year by year, it is not so obvious why extra funds have been granted to Haberdashers' CTC which is already operating at full capacity.[2]

Defenders of CTCs can point to the marked inequalities which have persisted in the funding of secondary schools even within the same LEA. But in the case of CTCs, matters are further complicated by the contributions which sponsors have been willing and certainly encouraged to make beyond their stake in the initial capital costs. Thus the first issue of Dixon's newsletter notes that its private funding considerably exceeded the basic building costs, thereby enabling it to be 'experimental and innovative to an extent which has previously been possible only in the private sector'. In an earlier appeal by its project director, it was made explicit that the projected annual grant from the DES would not 'cover fully the costs of running the number of specialised computers or the technological bias' and that assistance was therefore being sought (described as 'investment, not gifts') in the form of seconded staff, equipment and materials. The extent of such help varies considerably between CTCs. By the time of our visits, Macmillan had received very little; Djanogly's lead sponsor had paid for an extensive CD-ROM network believed to outmatch anything in universities or polytechnics in the region; Djanogly CTC has a 'state-of the-art' foreign language laboratory largely funded by a local company, and sophisticated enough to be booked by other local firms; and Brooke CTC claimed a 'state-of-the-art' sound system donated by an electronics firm which is one of its sponsors. Of course, CTCs' typical IT allocation of £250,000 each makes them not only 'interesting' to suppliers (Denholm 1991) but also quite likely to attract 'gifts' of equipment to such evident showpieces – as 'Education 2000' attracted support from Research Machines and Digital. But while evidence of gifts and 'investments' can be found in maintained schools too, the prominence of sponsorship in the CTC initiative makes it inappropriate that it has not been monitored more systematically either by the DES or the Trust. The consequent lack of information makes it even more difficult to assess the validity of claims for and against financially favourable treatment.

The main argument in defence of CTCs is that the necessary condition for successful innovation is not exceptional funding but the freedom from LEA 'control' which gives exceptional scope for innovation. As Kenneth Baker put it to us:

> They are going to be some of the most successful schools there are. Now the critics will say – 'Ah well, they're bound to be because you've thrown money at them, you've built new premises, you've equipped them marvellously. But it's not just that. Look at the tremendous capital investment in ordinary state schools . . . and it hasn't gelled. Not in all cases, there are some excellent state schools, but it hasn't gelled because the magic wasn't there, the music wasn't right. And the music is *right* with these schools – because you broke the system basically, they're outside the system. And you had a greater creativity.

A sense of being enabled to make radical changes by stepping outside the usual bureaucratic structures came through in many of our interviews with sponsors, project directors and principals. In the phrase which several used, it took too long in LEA settings to 'turn the tanker around'. Susan Fey put that view strongly when we spoke with her in 1989:

> CTCs are new and unique concepts but they're not made up of new and unique concepts. Over the past few years we've had COMPACT schemes, TVEI, industry–school links. The problem is that when you're trying to do these in an existing very bureaucratic structure, they tend to remain on the margins. And I think what CTCs are doing is saying – 'That's really good, let's put it in the central core'. . . . That's the unique thing in my opinion. . . . I've been in local authorities for over twenty years – good, bad and indifferent ones – and I'm convinced that we can't start something as completely new and innovative as a CTC is within a local authority structure . . . the structure itself prevents it from happening. You have to step outside to make it happen.

Looked at not as parts of a 'movement' but as independent schools, other commentators have seen in CTCs the 'freedom and flexibility of short chains of command' which made a fast pace of innovation possible (Regan 1990: 38), and as being enabled to demonstrate the benefits of that 'meaningful autonomy' – and the clear goals and strong leadership which are a consequence of it – which 'is not possible within the current education system' (Chubb and Moe 1992: 22).

We expressed in chapter 6 our scepticism about that claim. There is certainly a tendency among CTCs to exaggerate the 'blankness' of the sheet on which they are able to 'write' new forms of educational 'excellence'. While most enjoy the initial freedom of new schools from the tight constraints of inherited reputation, several are 'successor' schools shaped to some extent by their predecessors' status and success. The requirement that all CTCs must secure a balanced intake representative of their catchment areas reduces pressure to go for a particular market, but we have reported some evidence that their customers may be more conservative about the education they seek, and less inclined to welcome experiments, than the more innovative CTCs might wish. We have also commented on the extent to which CTCs represent a top-down initative, constrained by the requirements of the national curriculum and by a particular curriculum 'mission' rather than emerging 'of their own accord' and 'tapping into the needs and interests of parents' (Chubb and Moe 1992: 28). At least potentially they are also constrained by their sponsors, whose right to intervene is formally recognised in their position as trustees and governors and who have been encouraged by government to take a continuing active interest in the development of 'their' school. That constraint might be expected to have been made real in those CTCs associated with a vigorously entrepreneurial sponsor, and where the motives for sponsorship included (as we reported in chapter 3) an overtly expressed wish to be much more than a provider of funds. In practice, however, and although the hovering and often actual presence of a sponsor was evident in several of the CTCs we visited, we encountered few instances of unwelcome inter- ference. It seemed that the personal interest of a sponsor or sponsoring company was being held in check both by other heavy commitments and by a businesslike belief in executive responsibility.

As we have seen, the CTC Trust is adamant in not wishing to act as a surrogate LEA even if CTCs were dependent enough to wish it. But in so far as the CTCs' main paymaster is the government, their relationship with the DES may give some indication of how 'state-independent schools' relate to the state. The example is not altogether auspicious. Though a few CTC staff claimed to have found civil servants more helpful than they had found the Trust, we have already noted complaints about the funding formula, the underestimating of capital and depreciation costs, the restrictions on intakes and the illogicality of having catchment areas at all. These amounted to a more general feeling that the government had not fully recognised the innovativeness of its own creations. Thus one project director, after commenting on the rapid turnover among the officials with whom he had had to deal, went on to complain both of lack of experience in dealing directly with schools and the extent to which the DES branch was for ever looking over its shoulder at a Treasury preoccupied with precise heads of expenditure inappropriate to the CTC programme.

As a further and obvious source of constraint, the highly controversial nature of the initiative has subjected CTCs to unusually close scrutiny. In many of our interviews, CTC staff mentioned their wish for a 'right to fail' which seemed a necessary condition for truly innovative schools. Instead, they had to recognise that any failures would be picked up and used against them – as happened, for example, with the critical comments about technology embedded within a generally favourable HMI report on Kingshurst. Since an eagerness for evidence of failure arises from hostility on principle to the whole CTC programme, it raises a further and fundamental question about the intended 'beacon or lighthouse effect' of CTCs. Even if their funding and working conditions are not dismissed as too eccentric to be relevant to the system at large, how are any exemplary innovations to be disseminated? We therefore inquired within CTCs about mechanisms for doing so, and about what they perceived as the main obstacles. Visiting maintained schools in CTC catchment areas, we asked about contacts with these new competitors and about any changes in policy or practice which might have been influenced by the CTC example.

To the extent that CTCs do indeed 'break the mould', then the likelihood of their achievements filtering through to neighbouring' schools is greatly diminished by the hostility which continues to surround most of them. As in other aspects of their development, however, generalisation is impossible. In Croydon, Wandsworth and Dartford, the CTCs were promoted or supported by the LEA and have not generally faced the strong formal inhibitions on contact with a 'maverick' institution which are evident in other areas and conspicuous in Middlesbrough, Nottingham and Gateshead. The consequences in that last area were clearly described by a senior executive from one of the CTC's sponsoring companies:

In theory . . . you set up a new CTC which you talk about as being a centre of excellence and something which other schools in the area will seek to emulate. Now that's fine in principle . . . but it doesn't work out like that because the local authority has gone out of its way to be uncooperative, they haven't helped to create an environment where that sort of support can be given. They've made it quite clear that they will not expect any of their teaching staff to apply for jobs at Emmanuel College and they would positively discourage them from doing so. . . . Now I believe that notwithstanding that local hostility . . . that there will be many teachers in the area who will look very carefully at Emmanuel College and will be encouraged by what they see and what they hear. . . . So one would hope that the beacon of excellence idea will apply, but I think it's going to take some time for it to work out, I think they're going to have to earn the right to be there. . . . It's all very well people like Kenneth Baker at the outset saying, 'These will be beacons of excellence'. They've got to earn that tag.

But being perceived as having earned it by nearby schools is certainly made more difficult by the extent to which CTCs are seen as privileged institutions, as intruders in local systems of secondary schooling which did not 'need' them, and of course by political objections to the wider education policy of which they are a part. The welcome given by Leigh CTC to visits from staff from other schools on professional development days would not be sought or allowed in other LEAs. In that particular area, the move towards grant-maintained status in other local schools may also have removed some of the inhibitions.

However, CTC teachers in other areas described the continuing hostility and suspicion with which they felt themselves regarded at local teachers' meetings, which they continued to attend so as to retain what links they could. A position of 'spendid isolation' is not only professionally uncomfortable, but also unacceptable in principle because of the 'beacon' role which has been accepted so eagerly. In terms very similar to those cited early in chapter 5, one principal stated firmly that:

My roots are very deliberately in state education. I do regard the legitimate role of CTCs as the research and development arm of *state* maintained education and on that basis my belief is that you can actually justify half a dozen, maybe ten, twelve, fifteen institutions that work with research partners. . . . What you are now seeing is CTC principals from within the movement – I *do* regard myself as being involved in a radical movement – and I think it is the CTC principals who are actually shifting the agenda and I don't think it was regarded as a legitimate function at the beginning. . . . The principals feel much more comfortable with the legitimate role being R&D than the all-singing, all-dancing, all-overclaiming role of CTCs. My view is that if we overclaim and talk about showering our beacon of excellence on to desperately under-funded inner city schools that are actually not taking only well-motivated students across the ability range, as we're seeking to do, but taking de-motivated students across the ability range, this is the elitist charge that we have to live with. So my view is that the ground has been shifted by CTC principals. . . . How could you expect all the ex-ILEA teachers who fetched up in the CTC movement to turn their backs on all the exciting development work that was being done in the inner cities?

Yet even if the CTCs were to become centres of innovation for what this principal terms 'the achieving school movement', the dissemination of what might be learned from their licensed experimentation seems problematic given the resentment at that licence. Even the sympathetic LEAs have made little systematic effort to include the CTCs in their overall development planning, the sharing of facilities between Croydon College and the Performing Arts and Technology School being a rare example of the sort of co-operation envisaged by the DES in 1986. It remains to be seen how far the 'principles and best practice' of CTCs will be extended through the conversion of maintained schools 'into schools with similar characteristics', and how far CTCs can be included (as they would wish) in the whole network of diversified local provision. Among the principal reasons behind Sir Cyril Taylor's wish to see CTCs extend into the main system in voluntary-aided and grant-maintained form was a wish to see their educational characteristics diffused more easily. Describing himself to us as 'a local government man by origin', he went on to balance against the advantages of independence the costs to a school's relations with its neighbours. There were also distinct advantages, he thought, in being 'in the family of the LEA'.

> If headteachers of comprehensive schools are regularly meeting through the LEA network with headteachers of voluntary-aided CTCs, they'll feel much less threatened and there'll be more co-operation, and the resources of the CTCs, the IT resources, will be available for other schools.

How far, if at all, the independent CTCs are part of their local networks varies greatly with the locality. One CTC might have 'more links with comprehensives than we've got with Eton', as its principal put it, because the LEA encouraged them and because he felt able to claim growing interest from rank-and-file teachers even in unsympathetic boroughs. But he regarded his CTC as 'an extreme example of co-operation', and it is hard to see how the 'beacon effect' can be significant without greater integration into those very LEA networks which they were partly designed to outflank. If other policies lead to the demise of LEAs, of course, entirely new means of networking among schools will need to emerge. Leigh CTC is already considering franchising parts of its post-16 curriculum to local grant-maintained schools. Whether such a client relationship will be acceptable to schools that are in direct competition with CTCs remains to be seen.

In the section that follows we look in more detail at the impact of CTCs on an existing network of schools. Before doing so, we consider briefly some potential effects which might be considerable even without open channels of communication. For example, being in competition with such apparently well-resourced schools might be expected to affect what other schools do and the way they market themselves. As a Kingshurst parent remarked:

> Since the CTC's been opened, every year when it's been coming up to children going into secondary schools we've had the leaflets coming through the door, you know, of all the surrounding schools. Now we never ever had that until the CTC opened. ... They weren't really interested then 'cos they thought, 'well, they haven't got a choice, so they'll send their children here and that's it'. But now they've got to fight for the children to go, they've got to show them what's on offer, which I think competition is good in anything.

She was not alone in ascribing changes in the attitudes of schools to the appearance of a CTC competitor rather than to a broader emphasis generally on school choice, and Kingshurst's principal has cited such views among Solihull parents as evidence of the beneficial effect of CTCs on the system as a whole (*BBC Radio 4* 6 June 1989). Certainly, schools in the catchment areas of CTCs might be expected to respond in terms of publicity and marketing to their new (and glossily presented) competitors, but our own visits to comprehensive schools in such areas produced slight evidence of such direct effects. Heads usually seemed far more aware of their comprehensive school competitors in the new conditions of open enrolment. As one commented:

> I have been much more conscious of marketing the school in the last three or four years than I suspect I have ever been in the past in terms of producing the standard sort of glossy brochure, but I haven't gone and stood in front of the station or put adverts in the local press yet.

Similarly, an independent school head told us:

> What is happening is much broader than CTCs – with LMS and GM schools – and gradual. Schools are going to have to market themselves and justify themselves – CTCs are only part of that and not dominant.

Nevertheless, as we described earlier, some CTCs have engaged in very direct selling, whether to establish their presence or to reach the kinds of pupils they felt needed them most. More conscious of that kind of competition, another comprehensive school head described his 'heavier' marketing as a matter of

> presenting ourselves as what we are – a small caring school – and we'll continue to present ourselves like that, keep our booklets smart and get as many as we can. We're not trying to compete and pretend we can offer anything in terms of resources to compare with the CTC.

While his response may appear consistent with the government's encouragement for diversity and specialisation in schooling, the refusal to compete with the CTC on its own terms suggests that the contribution of competition to school improvement is likely to be more complex and indirect than is often implied by the advocates of competition and choice.

IMPACT ON LOCAL PROVISION

The CTC initiative was always intended to help transform the public sector by enhancing choice and diversity, rather than merely to provide an escape route from it. The Assisted Places Scheme had also been defended as shaking up a complacent system, but its main justification was as a ladder for able children. With CTCs, the emphasis on systemic effects has been much stronger and much more explicit. Within the political frame of reference from which they emerged, CTCs were intended to typify the benefits of liberating the supply side of education from the LEAs' 'monopoly', and demonstrate the capacity of 'independent' schools to outperform those 'shackled' by LEA control. It is hardly surprising, then, that LEA hostility has been dismissed as the defensive reaction of producer interests under threat. As Chubb and Moe put it, CTCs were 'an anti-system reform', and so were inevitably opposed by defenders of the system (1992: 24). But there are more specific reasons for that hostility, most obviously the perceived absurdity of creating new school places in the very areas most likely to have surplus places already.

Like the earlier introduction of assisted places, the CTC programme aroused immediate protests about undermining and 'creaming' maintained schools whose viability would thereby be put at risk. But in this case the threat seemed much greater because it was so much more concentrated. Among the ostensible purposes for defining 'substantial' catchment areas was to avoid too much pressure on particular schools, though we saw earlier that the Association for Science Education (1986: 3) noted a 'striking similarity' between them and 'the domain from which a typical grammar school population was drawn'. The main problem arose because the siting of CTCs where education was 'under most pressure' placed them in areas where secondary rolls had fallen sharply. Eight of the directors of education we interviewed commented on the absurdity of creating new thousand-strong CTCs in areas where they had struggled to rationalise secondary provision under government pressure (reinforced by Audit Commission evidence) to cut the cost of unneeded places. Indeed, if more CTCs had been created in the locations favoured by the government in 1986, this difficulty would have been exacerbated. Of those we interviewed, only the directors of Croydon and Wandsworth – both flagship Conservative boroughs which had already made large cuts in their school capacities – argued that a well-run LEA ought to be able to overcome the logistic problems involved. Yet, in Wandsworth, the LEA successfully opposed an application for grant-maintained status from a school designated for closure, while permitting an already-closed school to reopen as a CTC. A much more representative view is conveyed by Gateshead's director:

So, we've got 15,000 secondary places and by 9 September 1990 there will be just over 9,000 children to go in those places. So we've got to strip out according to Circular 3/87 two-fifths of those places. What then happens is that potentially 1,000 places get put back in. Again, the logic of that escapes me. Even if the net is spread widely, I can't see it [the CTC] as having much less of an effect than say 500 places being put back into the Gateshead system . . . then effectively you are talking about taking another school out of the system more than we had expected. . . . So that you will, in effect, replace an LEA maintained school by the CTC.

He went on to comment on the irony of Gateshead's having received from the Department of Employment ahead of time an extension of its TVEI programme because it was 'doing so well' at about the same time as another government department were deciding that something had to be done to improve the situation there 'so let's give them a CTC to compete with'.

Even if the need for a CTC could be accepted in some areas, they have certainly not, as we have seen, always been sited where conventional schooling is in obvious crisis and in need of a challenge. The further examples which follow are taken from one particular area in south-east London, and they may not therefore be typical of the effects of CTCs in all areas, but they do suggest that the introduction of a CTC can itself put the education service under pressures which will not necessarily prove to be beneficial. In particular, they illustrate how, whether deliberately or not, the CTC initiative has seriously undermined the planning role of the LEA.

As noted in chapter 3, the two Haberdashers' schools in Lewisham that were transformed into a CTC were widely regarded as being among the most successful comprehensive schools in the ILEA area. Lewisham LEA, as one of successor authorities to the ILEA, was regarded as more likely than many to succeed. At least until it suffered severe budgetary problems in 1990–1, it was rarely mentioned among those inner London LEAs that would have difficulty in providing an adequate education service. Nor, despite its Labour council, was it regularly pilloried in the popular press as a hotbed of 'loony Leftism'. Yet, as well as losing the two Haberdashers' schools to become CTCs, Lewisham was surrounded by the highest concentration of

CTCs in the country. Bacon's College was to its north in Southwark and Harris CTC not far to the south in Croydon. It was also in the likely catchment area of the Performing Arts and Technology School for pupils at 14 and 16-plus. We therefore tried to identify the impact of the CTC policy, and especially of the change of status of the Haberdashers' schools, on this particular LEA. It is difficult to overstate the potentially destabilising effect of what came as a major distraction just at the point at which Lewisham was seeking to establish itself as a new LEA. Visiting 'a very high-ranking official in the DES', a Lewisham officer

> expressed my concern about the proposal. I told him I didn't think it was appropriate and I said it was particularly difficult for us in the context of trying to get the new local authority off the ground. I also saw Susan Fey, the Executive Officer of the CTC Trust, and told her the same.

However, the Lewisham approach was not as confrontational as that adopted in some other Labour-controlled LEAs. Indeed, some discussion took place about a different model of a CTC in which the LEA would be an active partner. Yet when it seemed that the Haberdashers' Company and the government would go ahead with their own plans regardless, the LEA joined the ILEA in complex, lengthy and ultimately unsuccessful court cases, in which the proposal was challenged and compensation sought. The indignation aroused was similar to that felt in another LEA fighting a grant-maintained school proposal through the courts. As the Lewisham officer put it:

> I felt we had been extremely unjustly treated ... it all happened at the same time as the Avon case and the same contradiction is there. On the one hand, the secretary of state and the DES are forcing local authorities or expecting local authorities to reorganise, reduce surplus places, manage the system, and on the other, they are taking decisions elsewhere to unmanage it.

In particular, 'the removal of the two Haberdashers' schools from the local authority system would cause the collapse of the North Lewisham 6th Form Consortium ... because it just wouldn't survive without those two schools'. This hastened a plan, later abandoned in the light of a further change in government policy, to reorganise 16–19 education throughout the borough. The LEA's planning role was thus compromised by two successive aspects of central government policy. The head of one of the other schools in the consortium told us:

> It destroyed our consortium. We're now in quite a mess in terms of sixth form arrangements, if a sixth form college can no longer happen as a result of the [recent] government announcement [removing colleges from LEA control]. So, in fact, the kids here have suffered because of it all.

The LEA officer also expressed a more general fear that a CTC at Aske's would

> result in an increase in the inequalities that already exist in the schools system in Lewisham in that they would act as a magnet, be very highly resourced, there would be no control of their admissions policies by the borough, and that this would probably further downgrade some of the borough schools. . . . There's going to be enormous pressures on [one of the other schools] in terms of its survival in the next school year.

Although this would not be '*directly* as a result of the Aske's in that they are not going to increase their admissions numbers', the LEA's attempt to plan a reduction in surplus places was to be abandoned to the market in a context where the LEA felt that its own schools would not be competing on equal terms.

In some ways, the Lewisham case was unique in that the CTC proposal for the Haberdashers' schools was seen partly as a way of maintaining their elite status within the borough. Heads of other secondary schools were outraged at that choice for transformation into a CTC. As one of them commented:

> In the first proposals that came out, the one for round here was placed in the middle of North Peckham which is a difficult area which has not very good schooling. . . . While I disagreed with it philosophically, if it was going into a really deprived place and they really meant it was for those sorts of children, then one in a sense was not going to carp. When I heard it was the Aske's, I was absolutely astounded and horrified and really angry – and still am very angry.

As another head put it, 'Aske's has the gold star on it without ever having to prove anything and I think that comes from the reputation of the schools before they became a CTC'.

This interpretation was exacerbated by a widely held belief that the Haberdashers' Company wanted to get away from the LEA because its schools' admissions policies were coming under critical scrutiny. There had been long-standing suspicions that there was an over-representation of academically able and middle-class children at the two Haberdashers' schools. Whether or not these suspicions were well-grounded, the very fact that the schools were already perceived as selective within the borough reinforced the notion that the CTC itself would be a selective school in the traditional sense. The removal of two of the most successful schools from LEA control also called into question the status of the schools that were left behind. The controversy was fuelled by accusations that the first intake to the CTC had discriminated against Afro-Caribbean entrants. Figures reported to Parliament showed that, while 38 per cent of Asian applicants and 35 per cent of white applicants were accepted, only 21 per cent of Afro-Caribbeans secured places (*Education* 21 June 1991). However, the school argued that this resulted from a high rate of applications among Afro-Caribbeans and that the proportions admitted corresponded to DES criteria concerning the character of the catchment area.

Although the change of status of the Haberdashers' schools clearly affected the LEA's plans for the borough's education service as a whole, the impact of the CTCs on individual LEA schools in Lewisham is much more difficult to assess. Harris CTC was not seen as a significant threat by any school in Lewisham, unlike those in some of the other boroughs nearby, while views differed about the potential impact of Bacon's. Even though all the local LEA school heads we interviewed took a negative view of CTCs, some were inclined to see them as an irritating distraction rather than as a major threat, and to rate them rather low in their hierarchy of perceived troubles. As a head new to the borough put it in June 1991:

In the three year period [of your research] CTCs must have been a minor blip on the screen compared to the other things schools are dealing with on a daily basis ... Lewisham's budget crisis is the major preoccupation now.

Two other heads made similar general points in the same year, and also pointedly downplayed the direct effects of the CTCs on their own schools' pupil recruitment:

> We haven't seen ourselves as desperately threatened [by CTCs], we're a large successful school with good results. . . . Charge capping is a much more pressing and immediate issue than the CTCs. They may become increasingly irrelevant.

> Being a popular school, the CTC has not affected the number of students who have applied to come here, as far as I'm aware. . . . This year we're more oversubscribed than we were the previous year.

Yet, just a year later, the LEA was expressing concern about a loss of academically able band one pupils from one of these schools, especially pupils who had been offered places and then chosen to go out of the LEA system. This could not be attributed to CTCs alone, because a neighbouring borough now had many grant-maintained schools. However, there was certainly a feeling among the head of the less well-subscribed schools in Lewisham that, in so far as the Haberdashers' and Bacon's CTCs would act as magnets, they would be magnets with a repelling effect on the schools around them. 'Oversubscribed at the best of times', in their former guise as voluntary schools, they would further benefit from the extra publicity given to CTCs and from what was seen as unfairly generous funding. One head made a direct comparison between Lewisham's £5 million overspend and the £14 million reportedly going to Bacon's and added, 'It's one pocket at the end of the day'. Another described

> two ends of a spectrum . . . one with tons of money being piled in and the rest of the state schools, because of the recent financial situation with Lewisham, having everything taken away from them. And even though they have their reputations, and they will manage and they will strive to achieve, if you haven't got the basic resourcing, you can't actually compete. . . . I read somewhere in an article about all first-year students [in a CTC] will be provided with a lap-top computer. . . . I mean that is totally out of any concept of what we could possibly, possibly have here.

There was already some evidence of the CTCs attracting staff from other schools. Harris CTC had a policy of not paying anyone less for a job than was being paid elsewhere in the vicinity, and offered incentives to existing staff who attracted new support staff to the school. The head just quoted described having had a shortlisted candidate for a deputy headship cancel an interview because he was being interviewed at Bacon's for a director of studies post which offered not only more money but also 'various incentive allowances that there was absolutely no way I could compete with'. Though no LEA schools were reported as contemplating counter-measures, even where LMS afforded them some scope for doing so, he could see growing difficulties in competing for scarce staff when it was already expensive to move to London, and when the 'better working environment' of a CTC might well attract those who had no strong political, philosophical or educational objections to them. Furthermore, although the recession, and its effects on teacher supply generally, has probably staved off fierce competition between CTCs and other schools for staff, there is some evidence that the squeeze on resources and deteriorating conditions of work in LEA schools are actually reducing teachers' resistance to CTCs on political and philosophical grounds.

Perhaps the most extreme case we found was a former left-wing member of the Greater London Council now teaching in a CTC, his motives stemming from a combination of unemployment and a general disillusion with politics. But some teachers were clearly being drawn to CTCs by what they saw as an educationally enlightened environment with unusual opportunities for experiment. We have already noted significant resemblances between the kinds of curriculum and pedagogy that some CTCs are developing, and forms of progressive education found in certain well-known state comprehensives of the 1970s and 1980s (Moon 1983). Many of the ideas for enhancing achievement in CTCs are reminiscent of ideas promoted in the ILEA by its former chief inspector (ILEA 1984). Furthermore, although the ILEA has often been characterised by government ministers as a repository of worst practice, it has also proved a fertile recruiting ground for senior staff in some of the local CTCs. Lewisham, in particular, had provided the principal of the Performing Arts and Technology School and the deputy principal of Harris CTC. It was scarcely surprising that some of their former colleagues were now being attracted by the idea of joining them, especially when there was low morale where they were. As the head of a school that had already had staff head hunted told us:

> They're able to offer conditions – the resourcing for departments, equipment and facilities. Staff were quoting these and the LEA situation. . . . We have [also] had a lot of people look [at posts in CTCs] and say 'not yet'. It will depend what happens in the LEA sector. It's not a positive choice but a negative one.

A NEW HIERARCHY OF SCHOOLS?

Some commentators have suggested that the combined effects of such factors will help secure for CTCs a favourable place in an emerging hierarchy of schools. Even schools without the benefit of the pre-existing reputation of Haberdashers' seem destined to mark themselves out as superior to local LEA comprehensive schools. The high level of oversubscription to CTCs suggests that there is already a widespread perception that they offer significant advantages over other local schools. We saw in chapter 4 that some of the parents at Kingshurst regarded the arrival of the CTC as restoring or even improving upon the old grammar school system, with any form of selective school apparently seen as superior to the local comprehensives.

We also saw that some parents at both Kingshurst and Harris saw CTCs as the next best thing to an independent school, though heads of nearby independent schools were not conscious of any significant impact of CTCs on their recruitment and they did not yet seem to regard them as competitors in the same market. As the head of an academically selective Croydon independent school put it:

> We have a record number of applications. On the surface it hasn't touched us remotely. It shouldn't, because the purpose of a CTC must reflect the full range of ability and we are serving a wider catchment area.

However, he did predict that, as a result of the broader shift toward self-managing schools:

> We will have to work harder, conscious of the fact that people will be fighting harder and presenting schools better, and hopefully running them much better. Better non-fee-paying schools will be more competition.

Walford and Miller have suggested that CTCs will join grant-maintained schools as part of an elite state sector and that they may even wish to move further 'up-market' as they become established. They argue that, in order to do this, CTCs may have to deviate from 'their role as centres of excellence for technology ... as Kingshurst already appears to be doing' (Walford and Miller 1991: 165). In this connection, we witnessed a fascinating disagreement between two government officials as to whether it would be a mark of success or failure if CTC principals were to be admitted to the Headmasters' Conference, the body that represents elite academic independent schools.

Given their growing popularity as a result of publicity and high levels of funding, there is certainly scope for the CTCs to screen their entries even more rigorously than they have to date. However, academic and social selection on grammar or elite independent school lines would require not only a reduced emphasis on their core mission in relation to technology, but also a considerable easing of the constraints on their selectiveness referred to in chapter 4 – a proposal that has already been floated by some leading members of the CTC movement. Without such a change and despite their current market appeal, it is not entirely clear that CTCs will become firmly entrenched at the top of the hierarchy, especially given that other schools are not subject to the same rigorous constraints on admissions and that comprehensive grant-maintained schools are now to be permitted to apply to change their character and become selective.

Despite current parental views about the standing of CTCs in the hierarchy, one principal told us that he was very concerned about the way in which the publication of test scores and examination results would impact on the public perception of CTCs. Schools such as Harris and Leigh will have to struggle hard to prevent the examination results of their pre-CTC intakes affecting parental perceptions of the quality of the education on offer, though others, such as Haberdashers', might benefit from the results of the sorts of pupils they had attracted in pre-CTC days. It is also questionable whether parents' high expectations of CTCs will be met even by the genuine CTC intakes, given the requirements about span of ability they have to meet. As long as the current restrictions on their intakes are maintained, CTC principals are likely to favour the publication of results on a 'value-added' basis rather than raw scores. All the principals expect CTCs to do relatively well with the sorts of intakes they get, but any expectation that results will compare with those of grammar schools or even successful comprehensives with middle-class intakes are regarded as ludicrously optimistic.

Nevertheless, for the present, there is considerable evidence in our interviews with parents, and with maintained school heads, to suggest that CTCs are widely perceived as offering significant advantages, real or imagined, to the pupils attending them. Indeed, even those of our respondents who were critical of the impact of CTCs on the system as a whole often recognised their attractions and the individual benefits they could offer. It therefore seems likely that this 'halo effect' will give CTCs a continuing market advantage over local LEA schools, even if the current restrictions on their admissions policies remain in place. Proposals, such as those being floated at Leigh, to franchise elements of its post-16 curriculum offer to local grant-maintained schools could also help to bolster the position of a CTC in the local hierarchy of schools.

EXTENDING THE CTC MODEL

Even supporters of the CTC initiative are wary of claiming that its success or failure can be judged in terms of its individual benefits alone. It is partly for this reason that the government has sought to extend some aspects of the CTC model throughout the system. Yet, although CTCs were created explicitly as a new kind of school, it was unclear at the outset whether the pilot network was intended to be followed by a much larger number of similar creations or whether it was intended to lead the way to a system of secondary schooling diversified into a variety of new forms. That uncertainty reflects the different policy strands identified in our opening chapters.

If they were primarily to pioneer a modern, technologically-oriented version of secondary education relevant to the presumed needs of employers and to alleviating critical skills shortages, then twenty CTCs could have only very limited effect unless great confidence was placed in them as beacons. As we have seen, both Cyril Taylor and Bob Dunn had envisaged at least one specialised 'technical' school developing in every LEA.

Professor Sig Prais called for an ambitious programme of a thousand or more such schools to 'improve the number and quality of our engineering technicians and craftsmen' and to increase the intake to technological courses at 16 (*Times Educational Supplement* 9 March 1990).

As a challenge to the LEA 'monopoly', and to the low standards attributed to it, the initial programme was also too limited. We have seen how the high unit costs needed to launch it aroused persistent and strident complaints that, to quote ICI's former education liaison officer, it was unacceptable to 'set up islands of affluence in a sea of underprovision and then claim that somehow the majority will benefit from the privileges conferred on the few' (*Times Educational Supplement* 6 October 1989). A large-scale expansion of the programme would be a defence against those objections, and would also alleviate what Sir Cyril Taylor referred to at interview as the 'embarrassing popularity' of the original CTCs.

However, such a solution was clearly impossible within the original funding formula. The perceived solution was therefore to transform more existing schools into something resembling CTCs in their specialised curriculum. One possible solution was to create grant-maintained CTCs, through linking the 1988 Act's grant-maintained and CTC clauses. However, this was felt by Taylor to require legislative changes. Another more immediate way forward, although it deviated from a key element of the original model, was through co-operation in funding between LEAs and (at a much reduced level of capital contribution) private sponsors. The conversion of some voluntary-aided schools into a new version of the model was therefore described by schools minister Angela Rumbold as 'one of the best ways we have come up with to spread the message' because it did not 'imply the enormous imput of resources that we had with the first CTCs' (*Guardian* 13 March 1990).

She had made the same point at a conference on CTCs organised the previous day by the Centre for Policy Studies. At that conference, Sir Cyril Taylor argued similarly that while twenty 'orthodox' CTCs had been necessary to prove the initiative's worth, and there had never been confirmed funding for more than that, the voluntary-aided route made it possible to transform an existing school for no more than £1 million for re-equipment and a transitional grant. If the conversion of an existing school could be done for £1 million compared with the £8 million–£9 million spent on a new CTC, and if the conversion costs could themselves be shared, then a multiplication of the original model was feasible. It was also highly desirable. Taylor argued 'better sixteen voluntary aided than one orthodox CTC' (*Times Educational Supplement* 19 January 1990) and, as a prominent proponent of the 'beacon' effect, he explained to us:

> I wouldn't have spent three years of my life, and sponsors wouldn't have put in their time and money into it, and secretaries of state put their prestige on it, for just twenty schools. It would be ludicrous. . . . What we're after is that if these [what he called 'new model CTCs'] work, and we can convince LEAs that they work, then the twenty grow until you have as many down the road as parents want to send their kids to. But you've got to start somewhere.

He also thought that the Catholic Church leaders who had opposed a normal CTC project would welcome the voluntary-aided route. The original programme was therefore no more than the start and the government's commitment to expanding the programme was increasingly couched in terms of developing the less expensive option of voluntary-aided and grant-maintained CTCs.

Taylor envisaged that another eighty CTCs could be created through the voluntary-aided mechanism. This could have helped realise his 1986 proposal that each LEA should have at least one new technical school to act as a catalyst for change. However, the lack of careful preparation and planning that, as we saw in chapter 3, had characterised the CTC initiative as whole was also evident in the implementation of this 'new direction'. In April 1990 Wandsworth announced plans to close Battersea Park School and reopen it as the first voluntary-aided CTC with its sponsors having to contribute much less than the 20 per cent stake of the earlier model. The plans were soon disrupted by the withdrawal of the original sponsor, ADT, and salvaged only by Sir Cyril Taylor's own company stepping in to fill the breach. Then, at a late stage, and after an apparent change of position at the DES, the proposal to use the voluntary-aided school regulations had to be shelved on the grounds that it would be unlawful for the LEA to hand over the buildings to the governors free of charge or to lease them at a peppercorn rate. It was decided that new legislation would be needed to remove any ambiguities about the legality of such proposals.

Meanwhile, however, the model has been extended in other ways. The CTC initiative does seem to have helped to place the idea of specialist provision on to LEAs' own agendas in some areas. As well as welcoming a conventional CTC and planning a voluntary-aided one, Wandsworth proposed a much broader plan to make each of its comprehensives a form of magnet school with up to £1 million cash injection. Strong local resistance to the proposals led to headteacher protests at a lack of consultation which culminated in a declaration of no confidence in the director of education, Donald Naismith. Nevertheless, parts of the proposal went ahead, including considerable LEA investment in technology facilities at Battersea Park School. Kent County Council announced the conversion of Geoffrey Chaucer School into a CTC-style school with £500,000 money from the LEA supplemented by private sponsorship. It claimed to be an obvious site for such an initiative because of its post-war pioneering of technical schools. A magnet scheme for Bradford was abandoned, again after strong protests from local headteachers, only when the Conservatives lost control of the council. In Lincoln, which was once considered a potential site for a CTC, the Lincoln School of Science and Technology opened in 1992 as a partnership between the county council and local business sponsors, with a £3.5m investment from the LEA and £300,000 from the sponsors. Lincolnshire, like Wandsworth, is an authority which is often seen as a testbed for future national policies for specialisation and diversity and nearly half of its secondary schools have gone grant maintained with LEA support.

In December 1991 the government gave further encouragement for the development of technology schools in every area, by announcing a Technology Schools Initiative. According to the DES press release, this demonstrated the government's commitment to 'the encouragement of greater diversity in the range of schools from which parents can choose' and was intended to 'give those schools who wish to specialise in technology the means to become a technology school'. Targeted at schools wishing to develop their teaching of technology with a vocational and practical orientation and make links with business and industry, it was anticipated that some of them would wish to 'take on the key characteristics of CTCs more generally' (DES 1991). To this end, £25 million of capital funding was to be made available in 1992–3 for LEAs and schools to bid for, £10 million of which was earmarked for grant-maintained and voluntary-aided schools. The expectation was that 100 successful schools would each receive support of around £250,000 for purchasing equipment and upgrading technology facilities.[3] Although the government claimed that this would allow schools 'to enhance their technology and related areas of the curriculum very significantly', even the usually loyal Wandsworth LEA responded by suggesting that this sum was too low to produce the necessary changes.[4] Certainly the scale of the funding is considerably less lavish than that invested in the original CTCs.

CTCs AND THE 1992 WHITE PAPER

Even these modest developments can be seen as contributing to the larger objective of creating a more diversified and specialised system of secondary education. As Caroline Cox put it, 'you've got to have choice between genuine alternatives, choice implies diversity' (quoted in Ball 1990: 44). Asked by us what would be different about CTC-style schools if they were spread more widely through the system, Sir Cyril Taylor answered:

> I think a specific educational focus. . . . And I think that one of the problems a comprehensive has – this confused egalitarian ideal which is thought can only be delivered by a uniform, homogeneous structure. I think some diversity of provision is critical, because kids do want different kinds of education and parents also want that.

Although a technology bias was an obvious attraction for sponsors anxious about their future recruitment of skilled workers, it was only part of what he saw as a broader diversity.

In the White Paper produced by John Patten, who became Secretary of State for Education immediately after the 1992 general election, CTCs were given a key role in what had now become an explicit policy of promoting specialisation and diversity in schools. The White Paper sought to bring together the various earlier initiatives, show how they would contribute to a 'new framework for schools' and set out the legislative changes that would be necessary to bring in the new order. It stated that

- The Government wishes to promote much greater diversity and specialisation by schools, particularly in technology, while still ensuring that the full National Curriculum is offered to all pupils
- The developing network of specialist Technology Schools, with CTCs at its centre, will be extended through the Technology Schools Initiative
- LEA maintained and GM schools will be able to form partnerships to operate as GM and voluntary aided Technology Colleges with private sector persons or organisations, who will be entitled to formal representation on the governing body
- LEAs will be able to contribute towards governors' capital costs at Technology Colleges and other voluntary aided schools.

(DFE 1992: 45)

The fifteen existing CTCs would thus be at the centre of an expanding network of specialist schools. Their role was explained as follows:

These CTCs have been established, in partnership with business, to implement an innovative curriculum with a particular emphasis on technology and science, aided by the widespread use of information technology, and to develop new school management practices.

(DFE 1992: 45)

Their progress to date was described thus:

They are proving outstandingly popular with parents in the inner city areas they serve; and they are already demonstrating new ways of motivating and enhancing the performance of pupils of all abilities. The Government will continue to look at the CTC programme as an important means of stimulating innovation and excellence in education.

(DFE 1992: 45)

This seemed to recognise the role of existing CTCs as research and development centres for the network as a whole and did not entirely rule out the possibility of new CTCs in the future. Meanwhile, joining the network would be the schools participating in the previously announced Technology Schools Initiative. In addition, the government also announced that it would resuscitate its plans for voluntary-aided and grant-maintained technology colleges. In order to overcome the earlier legal objections, the government is now planning to legislate to permit existing grant-maintained and voluntary-aided schools to develop in this way by enabling both the secretary of state and LEAs to contribute towards governors' capital costs at voluntary-aided schools. Such schools will be able to seek business sponsors and appoint them to their governing bodies, as will existing grant-maintained schools. LEA maintained schools will be able to apply to become grant-maintained technology colleges and it will also be possible to establish new voluntary aided technology colleges. Unlike CTCs, these institutions will not be confined to urban areas and they might choose to place an emphasis on technology within modern languages or business studies, rather than science and technology or the performing arts. The intention is that these changes, along with others further reducing the role of LEAs, will be put into effect in an education Bill brought before Parliament in the 1992–3 session. The CTC concept seems, then, about to be generalised even before its impact has been properly evaluated.

Chapter 7

New schools for new times?

This book has been concerned with a policy that has so far produced only fifteen schools, and it might reasonably be asked why we have given so much attention to so limited an initiative. Further point was given to this question during the course of our research when Jenny Ozga (1990) argued that, while such studies of individual policies might provide rich descriptive data, they could also obscure the 'bigger picture' when trying to make sense of contemporary education policy.

Throughout the book, we have tried to understand CTCs in terms of their relationship to the government's education policy as a whole. As we saw in chapter 6, in the light of the 1992 White Paper on the future shape of the education system, it now makes sense to see the prototype CTCs not only alongside the newer forms of CTC and the Technology Schools Initiative, but also in the context of a changing approach to the governance of schools more generally (DFE 1992). Although the scale of public and private investment in the original CTCs is unlikely to be repeated elsewhere, many of the features of CTCs are now to be spread much more widely – and thinly? – throughout the education service.

However, if our main emphasis has been on the relationship between CTCs and other aspects of recent education policy, we also argued in chapter 1 that CTCs needed to be seen as part of a broader project on the part of the Conservative government in Britain. Even if, in the past, education policy had sometimes seemed to enjoy a degree of autonomy from other areas of policy-making, a strong commitment on the part of the Thatcher government to common policies – particularly those designed to enhance consumer choice – has produced a closer articulation between education and other fields of policy.

However, it may be that CTCs are part of a movement that is much broader and deeper than the particular set of policies that we have come to term 'Thatcherism'. In this final chapter, we therefore consider how far it is useful to draw upon some of the concepts of contemporary social, economic and political theory to make sense of CTCs as part of that 'bigger picture'. We consider in turn how far CTCs and related reforms can usefully be understood as part of an attempt to foster a market in welfare services, as a product of the changing relationship between the institutions of the state and civil society, as a parallel to similar changes taking place elsewhere in the world, as a response to deeper shifts in patterns of production and consumption and, finally, as an expression of that rather ill-defined constellation of changes that is sometimes taken to signal that we are now living in a 'post-modern' age. While accepting that such concepts can provide some useful insights into the broader significance of the CTC policy, we go on to argue that it is important to recognise some strong continuities between current policies and traditional patterns of educational inequality in England.

MARKETISING WELFARE?

We have already seen that it is possible to mount a strong case that the CTC policy needs to be understood within the broader context of Thatcherism. The announcement of the CTC initiative coincided with the inauguration of a more radical move in the direction of a market-oriented welfare system than had been evident during the first two periods of Mrs Thatcher's administration. While the private welfare sector expanded during that period and the public sector was increasingly under-financed, the structure of the latter remained largely unchanged. Some of the ideas informing CTCs, which were more clearly evident in the Education Reform Act, foreshadowed a more general thrust towards the creation of what Le Grand (1991) has termed quasi-markets in key areas of social welfare, notably education, housing, health and 'community care' during Mrs Thatcher's third term of office.

While the state has continued to finance provision in these areas, the system of provision has begun to be reformed. The essence of the reforms has been a shift away from centralised, collectivist, needs-led planning towards a market-led, devolved system of welfare based on the principle of 'consumer sovereignty'. On the demand side, services 'users' have become 'consumers' with the 'freedom' to choose between competing suppliers of welfare. The deregulation of the supply side has supposedly involved giving the providers of welfare the incentive and independence to become more responsive to what consumers want.

In this context the CTC initiative can be seen as a preliminary attempt to recast the state welfare user as a consumer and to make state welfare producers more responsive to consumer demand. As we have seen, CTCs were presented as a new choice of school for parents in the inner cities whose children were supposed to have suffered most from monopoly LEA provision. Parallel developments have been taking place in housing. Throughout the 1980s and into the 1990s, the council housing sector was being consistently eroded through the right to buy and alternative landlord schemes, and the abolition of local authority subsidies for council rents. Particularly 'significant from the quasi-markets perspective is the gradual but accelerating phenomenon of the expansion of the housing association movement to supplant local authorities as the main new providers of social housing' (Le Grand 1991: 6). The expansion of the housing associations movement was the result of the Housing Act 1988 which allowed for the transfer of council housing to private landlords, housing associations or tenants' co-operatives. Housing associations can therefore be seen, in some senses, as the housing equivalent of CTCs or grant-maintained schools, even if the latter do not currently charge their clients the equivalent of rent. Johnson has commented that, although the housing policies undoubtedly represent choice for some tenants, choice for others is curtailed:

> Those who wish to become local authority tenants find that the best houses have been sold and, as the stock diminishes and fewer council houses are built, waiting lists and waiting times lengthen and exchanges for those already in council housing and remaining in it become more difficult.
>
> (Johnson 1990: 157)

Forrest and Murie, writing in 1988, predicted that 'the public housing sector is well on the way to becoming an unambiguosly residual, second class form of housing provision, serving the poorest sections of the population' (Forrest and Murie 1988: 83)

The parallels with the fears expressed by critics of the CTC policy, as reported earlier in this book, are obvious. And the parallels in policy development do not stop there. The Housing Act 1988 also introduced a housing version of the Education Associations which the 1992 education White Paper envisages 'rescuing' failing schools (DFE 1992). These took the form of Housing Action Trusts set up to take over run-down estates from local authorities.

We do not have space here to document the quasi-market reforms in health and 'community care' or the social services in any detail, but the same general principles underpin them. There is an emphasis on the family and 'the community' as the preferred sites of care, though the health quasi-market differs from those in education and housing in the sense that the individual 'consumer' is not the purchaser. Health 'products' are purchased from competing providers on behalf of individuals by fund-holding general practitioners and district health authorities. This means that individuals less able to 'work the system' are to some extent 'cushioned' more than is the case in education or housing. Nevertheless, despite these differences across the various sites, CTCs and subsequent education policies do appear to have some consistency with broader attempts to marketise welfare provision.

DEPOLITICISING EDUCATION?

At one level the marketisation and residualisation of welfare can be seen as part of a continuation of the retrenchment in public expenditure, particularly welfare spending, which followed the economic crisis of the mid-1970s. As Harvey explains in relation to parallel developments in Britain and the USA:

> The gradual withdrawal of support for the welfare state . . . and the attack upon the real wage and organized union power, that began as an economic necessity in the crisis of 1973–5 were simply turned by the neo-conservatives into a governmental virtue.
>
> (Harvey 1989: 169)

The attempt to transform national economies within a changing global economic context has certainly involved an attempt to transfer certain responsibilities and costs away from the state to civil society, most notably in Britain through the privatisation of state-owned utilities. It should be noted, however, that overall public expenditure in Britain increased during the Thatcher regime. From 1978/9 to 1989/90 it rose in real terms by 11 per cent, partly because of a rise in unemployment and partly because of increased spending on defence and law and order. Therefore, as Johnson (1990) has pointed out, what actually changed was the pattern of expenditure.

This has particular relevance in the case of education, where privatisation, in the economic sense of the term, has been of limited significance. What has been more in evidence has been a shift in the ways in which state-funded education has been provided and consumed. There has also been a shift in the way education is administered. Alongside, and potentially in place of, collective provision by elected bodies with a responsibility to cater for the needs of the citizenry, there are increasing numbers of quasi-autonomous institutions operating devolved budgets and competing for clients in the market-place. Thus, as we have seen, the CTC initiative introduced a new sector of schools into the state system, directly funded by the state but operating independently of LEAs; the Education Reform Act extended that sector by introducing grant-maintained schools; the 1992 White Paper aims to expand it even further.

Along with changes in the way the state regulates other areas of social activity, such as housing and health, the new administrative arrangements for managing education can be seen as new ways of resolving the problems of accumulation and legitimation facing the state in a situation where the traditional welfare state cannot deliver what it promises or resolve the contradictions between different functions of the state (Dale 1989). With the removal of tiers of government between the central state and individual institutions, conventional political and bureaucratic control by elected bodies is replaced by market accountability assisted by a series of directly appointed agencies, trusts and regulators. Although such developments are a move in the direction of a market-based pluralism, thorough-going market liberals like Stuart Sexton believe they do not go far enough. This is partly because the advocates of such new institutional arrangements are drawn from a wider constituency than neo-liberal market fanatics.

Chubb and Moe (1990; 1992) are among a growing number of commentators who argue that the combination of democratic control by elected bodies and the powerful bureaucracies they generate is a major cause of the poor performance of modern mass education systems. The new institutional arrangements that they propose make it appear that education has been removed from this political arena. Quasi-autonomous institutions with private and voluntary involvement in their operation, even when they are largely state funded, blur the boundary between the state and civil society and appear to make education less of a political issue. Part of the reason for the intense opposition to these policies by the educational establishment may be because they constitute an attempt to reposition education in relation to the state and civil society and because they also constitute an attempt to deny education's traditional claim that it is somehow a special case that needs to be administered differently from other services.

In practice, though, the education reforms in Britain are as much to do with transferring power from the local state to the central state as with giving automony to the schools. Riddell (1992) suggests that the likely outcome is that criticism of education that has hitherto been conveniently directed at LEAs will now fall squarely on central government. However, the rhetoric accompanying the reforms seeks to suggest that education has been taken out of politics. This was made explicit by the Secretary of State for Education, John Patten, when he argued, in launching the 1992 White Paper (DFE 1992), that one of its aims was to 'depoliticise' education by removing it from the local political arena and giving power to parents and school governors. The special status of education was also to be reduced by the removal of the statutory requirement on local councils to administer education through a dedicated education committee. At least in terms of the rhetoric, the developments of which CTCs and grant-maintained schools are a part are highly consistent with new ways of understanding and organising public institutions that are fast becoming an orthodoxy in many parts of the world (Dale 1992).

A GLOBAL MOVEMENT?

Thus, a further reason why CTCs might be thought to have significance far beyond their numerical strength lies in their similarity with recent reforms elsewhere. Not only is the rhetoric of the British government's 'five great themes' – quality, diversity, parental choice, school autonomy, and accountability (DFE 1992) – echoed in other countries (Whitty and Edwards 1992), there are also some specific policies with similarities to CTCs.

Initially we looked to magnet schools in the USA in order to understand the provenance of CTCs. We concluded that the relationship was a somewhat tenuous one in which a poorly understood policy was being used to legitimate a poorly thought out one. Yet, as we saw in chapter 2, a symbolic link was forged through Kenneth Baker's much-publicised 1987 visit to a succession of magnet and other specialist schools in the USA. Ministerial references to the example of German *Realschulen* had a similar effect, with the added advantage of citing a nation to whose economic success the school system was thought to have contributed greatly. Then, in 1991, George Bush launched the New American Schools' initiative, which, in turn, seemed to owe something to the CTCs: 535 New American Schools, one in each congressional district, were to be established by September 1996 through a unique partnership among 'communities, inventors, educators, and entrepreneurs . . . a new partnership between the private sector and government'. While these 'new' schools would differ from CTCs in a number of respects, not least the channelling of business investment into funding design teams rather than the sponsorship of individual schools, the similarities of the mission were also striking.[1] According to a New American Schools Development Corporation brochure circulated in 1991, New American Schools would help 'break the mold' of American education by challenging 'assumptions commonly held about schooling'.[2] These included the prevailing adherence to blackboards and chalk, a curriculum organised into subjects and class periods, the six-hour school day and the 180-day school year, technology located only in the computer lab and the principal's office, and policies that discouraged risk-taking and offered few rewards for improved learning. Breaking the school district monopoly in the provision of state education was also to be a key feature of the policy, with a range of organisations, institutions, agencies and individuals becoming eligible to receive federal funds to develop the new schools with assistance of the design teams.

Despite the similarities, a White House official denied any specific relationship between CTCs and the New American Schools initiative and judged CTCs to have been at most a very minor influence. Their relevance was recognised but, rather like magnet schools in relation to CTCs, as a source of confirmation rather than as a direct model:

> I remember at some point seeing an article that I put in a pile that I was going to read. . . . But I think the genesis of the idea came from a couple of different things, though I think it may have played a role. . . . [Education Secretary] Lamar Alexander's interest in it came from a pilot project in Tennessee where a Saturn car plant had worked to set up a school with some money in a district and worked with local innovators and so he saw the concept of a private sector school. In addition, we had a couple of states trying things and the Nabisco Twenty-first [Next] century schools project. . . . Also [Deputy Secretary] David Kearns . . . had some experiences at Xerox. . . . I think in one of the conversations somebody may have mentioned the goings-on out there [in the UK], but the model came from the States.

In this case (as in others), we concluded that policy-makers in both countries were working within similar frames of reference and producing parallel policy initiatives, rather than directly 'borrowing' policies one from the other.

In the case of the British and US central governments of the 1980s and early 1990s, this process was no doubt facilitated by the existence of a common policy community with a shared political philosophy (Whitty and Edwards 1992). However, this network factor is less convincing as an explanation of developments elsewhere. It is clear that support is being given to the diversification and specialisation of educational provision and to local control of schools from a variety of political perspectives, as well as in countries with different political regimes. Indeed, although school choice policies in the USA received particular encouragement from Republican presidents Reagan and Bush, the growth in site-based management policies, magnet schools, and other schools of choice has received much broader support. A market approach to education has now entered mainstream social thinking in the USA and is by no means narrowly associated with the New Right (Chubb and Moe 1990).

Furthermore, similar policies have been pursued by Labour governments in Australia. In New Zealand, where advocates of community empowerment united with exponents of consumer choice against the old bureaucratic order, a Labour government's moves in the direction of devolution and school autonomy prepared the ground for the market-oriented policies now being pursued by a right-wing government (Grace 1991; Gordon 1992). Meanwhile, in parts of Eastern Europe, the centrally planned education systems of the Communist regimes are also being replaced with experiments in educational markets. Finally, international organisations are now encouraging the introduction of similar policies into some of the less developed countries.

Even though these tendencies have certainly not penetrated all countries, and they have been mediated differently by the traditions of different nation states and different political parties, the similarity between British policies and those being introduced elsewhere suggests another reason why they may be more significant than they at first appear. This is that such policies may reflect deeper changes emerging within the world economy.

A FACET OF POST-FORDISM?

Some observers suggest that we are witnessing the transportation of changing modes of regulation from the sphere of production into other arenas, such as schooling and welfare services. Various commentators have pointed to a correspondence between the establishment of markets in welfare and a shift in the economy away from Fordism – the term often applied to the assembly line mass production of standardised goods. The shift has been described as follows:

> The post-Fordist mode of accumulation places a lower value on mass individual and collective consumption and creates pressures for a more differentiated production and distribution of health, education, transport and housing.
>
> (Jessop *et al.* 1987: 112)

It also involves a restructuring of the labour market into a core and periphery and new ways of organising the labour process making extensive use of the new technologies. Although not all exponents of the post-Fordist thesis would agree, some writers also detect a correspondence between the restructuring of the labour market and the political creation of 'two nations' (Jessop *et al.* 1987: 109).

It is possible, however, to overstate the dichotomy between Fordist and post-Fordist regimes of accumulation. As Rustin points out:

> It is far from clear how much of the emerging economic system fits this new pattern of technology and organisation, and how much still operates either in old 'mass production' modes, or still more technologically-backward methods dependent on unskilled labour. . . . What seems to be emerging is not one 'progressive' mode of information-based production, but a plethora of co-existing and competing systems, whose ultimate relative weight in the system is impossible to predict. Since socio-technical systems do not develop completely autonomously, but only in response to cultural definition, conflicts of social forces, and political decision, it is dubious in principle and possibly misleading in fact to make linear extrapolations from what might seem to be 'leading instances', or current trends, to the shape of a whole system.
>
> (Rustin 1989: 58)

Furthermore, some theorists prefer to characterise the changes in the economy as neo-Fordism rather than post-Fordism. As such, they see the changes as 'an *adjustment* to the problems of Fordism, a way forward that extends the period of Fordism' rather than a qualitatively new economic direction, or a *step beyond* Fordism into a new era, as implied by the concept of post-Fordism (Allen 1992: 193).

Despite these problems with the notion of post-Fordism, various observers have claimed to see in CTCs and other recent education policies discussed in this book a response to changes in the prevailing modes of capitalist production and consumption, reflecting a shift from the 'Fordist' school of the era of mass production to what Stephen Ball has termed the 'Post-Fordist school' (Ball 1990). The emergence of new sorts of schools may therefore be the educational equivalent of the rise of flexible specialisation in place of the old assembly-line world of mass production, driven by the imperatives of differentiated consumption rather than mass production. Jane Kenway summarises and develops Ball's argument as follows:

> educational institutions are not only to produce the post-Fordist, multi-skilled, innovative worker but to behave in post-Fordist ways themselves; moving away from mass production and mass markets to niche markets and 'flexible specialisation' . . . a post-Fordist mind-set is currently having implications in schools for management styles, curriculum, pedagogy and assessment.
>
> (Kenway 1992: 14)

CTCs would appear to be in the vanguard of such a shift, with their shopping mall or business park architecture, their 'flat' management structures, and their emphasis on 'niche marketing', all apparently offering support for what appears to be an updated version of the Bowles and Gintis 'correspondence thesis' (Bowles and Gintis 1976).

There are also potential parallels to be drawn between the management strategies of post-Fordist industries and those of CTCs. Post-Fordist business entrepreneurs typically achieve maximum flexibility by abandoning the old industrial sites in favour of greenfield locations:

> Here they can avoid or attempt to manipulate the unions in the process of asserting management's right to manage. . . . The green field sites also offer the entrepreneurs the chance to avoid those local councils who are likely to increase taxes on commercial and industrial land, readjust zoning regulations or bring in tighter pollution controls.
>
> (Watkins 1991: 217)

In a similar way Baker's CTC initiative, at least as initially conceived, facilitated greater flexibility for educational entrepreneurs. By virtue of direct state funding and greenfield locations beyond the control of local authorities, CTC project directors and principals could avoid the teacher unions' and the LEAs' 'restrictive practices'.

However, just as there are problems with the notion of post-Fordism as an entirely new regime of accumulation, there are a number of problems with the new correspondence thesis as applied to education. We need to be cautious in concluding from any parallels that may exist between economic and social modes of organisation that we are experiencing a wholesale move away from a mass-produced welfare system towards a flexible, individualised and customised post-Fordist one. In this field too, it is difficult to establish a sharp distinction between mass and market systems. In education, the so-called comprehensive system was never as homogeneous as the concept of mass-produced welfare suggests. Indeed, it was always a system differentiated by class and ability. What may be different in the new era is an intensification of these differences and a celebration of them in a new rhetoric of legitimation, involving choice, specialisation and diversity, to replace the previous language of common and comprehensive schooling.

A POST-MODERN PHENOMENON?

Jane Kenway (1992) has brought together a number of theories underlying the idea of 'new times' to argue that, in education as elsewhere, modern societies *are* now entering a qualitatively new era. She suggests that accounts that concentrate solely on institutional changes pay insufficient attention to other cultural shifts which help to explain why markets in education have found such a receptive audience. For Kenway, 'the rapid rise of the market form in education is best understood as a post-modern phenomenon' (Kenway 1992: 12). In post-modernity, the significant nexus is that between the global and the local, limiting even the scope of the national state. She sees the new technology as a key element in the development of new and commodified cultural forms. What she calls the 'markets/education/technology triad' is a crucial feature of post-modernity, a triad in which CTCs could clearly be located. Kenway's account of post-modernity is, as she readily admits, a pessimistic one in which 'transnational corporations and their myriad subsidiaries . . . shape and reshape our individual and collective identities as we plug in . . . to their cultural and economic communications networks' (Kenway 1992: 19). The picture is one in which notions of 'difference', far from being eradicated by the 'globalisation of culture', are assembled, displayed, celebrated, commodified and exploited (Robins 1991).

Yet there are other accounts of post-modernity where the rhetoric of 'new times' offers positive images of choice and diversity. In this context, CTCs and other current developments might be regarded as part of a wider retreat from modern, bureaucratised state education systems – the so-called 'one best system' in the USA, for example (Glenn 1988; Chubb and Moe 1990) – that are perceived as having failed to fulfil their promise and now seem inappropriate to the heterogeneous societies of the late twentieth century. Thus, part of the appeal of current education policies lies in the claim that different types of schools will be responsive to the needs of particular communities and interest groups that exist as a result of the complex patterns of political, economic and cultural differentiation in contemporary society which have replaced the traditional class divisions upon which comprehensive education was predicated. While this process of differentiation is partly about creating new markets for new products, the multiplicity of lines of social fissure that are emerging may be associated with deeper changes in modes of social solidarity. In so far as these divisions and associated identities are experienced as real, they are likely to generate aspirations that will differ from traditional ones.

This has contributed to more optimistic readings of post-modernity than the one to which Kenway subscribes. Compared with the oppressive uniformity of much modernist thinking, it is possible to regard post-modernism as 'a form of liberation, in which the fragmentation and plurality of cultures and social groups allow a hundred flowers to bloom' (Thompson 1992: 225–6). Thus, many feminists have seen attractions in the shift towards the pluralist models of society and culture associated with post-modernism and post-modernity (Flax 1987). The possibilities for community, rather than bureaucratic, contol of welfare are also viewed positively by some ethnic minority groups. In the USA, the recent reforms of the school system in Chicago sought to dismantle the vast bureaucracy under which the Chicago School District was perceived by many commentators to be failing the majority of its pupils even when controlled by black politicians. The devolution and choice policies were enacted as a result of a curious alliance between New Right advocates of school choice, black groups seeking to establish community control of their local schools, together with dis-illusioned white liberals and some former student radicals of the 1960s (Hess 1990).

Support for schools run on a variety of principles, rather than those of the 'one best system', might then be seen as recognising a widespread collapse of a commitment to modernity. Or, put another way, a rejection of the totalising narratives of the Enlightenment Project and their replacement by 'a set of cultural projects united [only] by a self-proclaimed commitment to heterogeneity, fragmentation and difference'; social development is no longer seen as 'the fulfilment of some grand historical narrative' but as 'a pragmatic matter of inventing new rules whose validity will reside in their effectivity rather than in their compatibility with some legitimating discourse' (Boyne and Rattansi 1990). The notion of 'unprincipled alliances', which at one time might have prevented such a political configuration as emerged in Chicago, is less appropriate in a context of post-modernity, which is seen by Lyotard (1986) as a pluralist, pragmatic and restless set of partially differentiated social orders. If large-scale attempts at social engineering have been perceived as failing, less ambitous aspirations may now be in order.

In Britain, the Labour Party's traditional social democratic policies have also been perceived as unduly bureaucratic and alienating by many black parents, who it is sometimes claimed welcome the new opportunities offered by the Reform Act to be closer to their children's schools (Phillips 1988). While they do not necessarily endorse the Thatcherite dream in its entirety, some aspects of it may well connect to the aspirations of groups who find little to identify with in the grand master narratives associated with class-based politics. Policies which seem to emphasise heterogeneity, fragmentation and difference may thus represent more than a passing fashion among neo-liberal politicians and resonate with changing notions of an open, democratic society as well as with a market ideology. Put in those terms, it is understandable that current policies have a potential appeal far beyond the coteries of the New Right.

Even on the Left, there has been some support for more specialised and diverse forms of secondary schooling. In *Parents in Partnership*, issued during the 1989 county council elections, the Labour Party proposed that schools should 'develop a distinctive character within the comprehensive principle'. The party considered using education support grants and local management of schools to encourage specialisation, with parents and children 'able to choose schools which offer the type of education most suitable to their interests and abilities' (*Times*

Educational Supplement 21 April 1989). The same idea was taken further by Peter Wilby who argued that 'young minds need magnets' (*The Independent* 15 June 1989) and that comprehensive schools had lost their way through being preoccupied with a balanced curriculum, which forced on the goats a second-rate version of what the sheep got. More curriculum specialisation was therefore desirable. While the idea of magnet schools remained highly contested, and failed to gain backing from the Labour front bench, a commitment to cultural diversity within the comprehensive principle did gain official acceptance through support for the development of Muslim voluntary-aided schools alongside those sponsored by the Anglican and Catholic Churches.

REWORKING OLD THEMES?

To some extent, CTCs and associated policies may then seem to be part of a wider set of changes. If we equate curriculum specialisation with niche marketing, CTCs appear to display some of the characteristics of post-Fordism, while their relationship to government is consistent with emergent forms of public administration more generally. Yet, notwithstanding Valerie Bragg's conscious attempts to make Kingshurst look more like a business organisation than a school (*BBC Radio 4* 6 June 1989), CTCs are still readily identifiable as secondary schools, with more similarities to local comprehensive schools than differences. This does not suggest a radical break with the concerns of modernity. Just as some commentators see changes in ways of managing production as neo-Fordism rather than post-Fordism – and new institutional forms as merely a new way of managing the modernist project – so much of CTC thinking can also be seen as a variation on a familiar theme. Furthermore, there are serious problems in trying to see the sort of diversity sponsored by CTCs and other recent reforms as a post-modern phenomenon in the strong sense of reflecting deep-seated changes in the nature of society. At most, CTCs lie at a point of tension between competing conceptions of contemporary social policy, as symbolised in the ongoing debate within the movement about the desirability of social engineered catchment areas in the context of markets and parental choice.

Some aspects of CTCs are the very epitome of the modernist project. This was apparent in the way their 'high tech' image was invoked in the early publicity. At least as much as comprehensive schools, CTCs seemed to express an underlying faith in technical rationality as the basis for solving social, economic and educational problems. Even in the new White Paper devoted to 'Choice and Diversity', this modernist project predominates. It is 'specialisation' rather than 'diversity' that is given prominence. Although the proposed legislation is to be 'drawn widely enough to encourage more schools to specialise in other fields too', the emphasis throughout is on technology, which will help 'to break down the divide between academic and vocational studies' and 'equip young people with the technological skills essential to a successful economy' (DFE 1992: 45). Indeed, the justification for specialisation is that 'other leading industrialised nations combine the attainment of high standards with a degree of specialisation' (DFE 1992: 43).

Furthermore, although CTCs may, as we suggested in chapter 4, have particular attractions for some members of the minority ethnic population, the ethos of CTCs is often assimilationist rather than one that actively fosters cultural pluralism. Indeed, one of the publicly made criticisms of Harris CTC by former Sylvan pupils was that 'they're leaving out the black people – in Sylvan they taught us about Rastas, black history and culture' (*Daily Telegraph* 4 July 1991). Although Muslim leaders have interpreted clauses of the 1992 White Paper as heralding the possibility of state-funded Islamic schools through the 'opting-in' of existing private schools (*Observer* 2 August 1992), the message in the White Paper is highly tentative and constrained:

> The Secretary of State . . . [will take steps that] will help to create opportunities for new GM schools to be created in response to parental demand and on the basis of local proposals.
> (DFE 1992: 26)

> The Government wishes to see the role of the Churches and other voluntary bodies in education preserved and enhanced.
> (DFE 1992: 32)

Certainly, the notion of curriculum specialisation, at least in technology, is much more clearly spelled out than that of diversity. Indeed, the chapter of the White paper entitled 'Specialisation and Diversity in Schools' is almost entirely about specialisation.

Nevertheless, the rhetoric of specialisation and diversity is given an added appeal by the suggestion that it will not entail selection and hierarchy. Early in our research, a former government minister characterised the drift away from comprehensive education towards more specialised and differentiated types of schools, not as a return to elitist approaches to educational provision, but as happening 'without any one [type of school] being regarded as inferior to the others' (Dunn, cited in *Education* 8 July 1988) – a situation which he apparently believed existed in Germany. Similarly, in the 1992 White Paper, the government stresses specialisation rather than selection and tells us that it is not its intention either to encourage or to discourage applications to make a school selective:

> The fact that a school is strong in a particular field may increase the demand to attend, but it does not necessarily follow that selective entry criteria have to be imposed by the school. The selection that takes place is parent-driven. . . . Parents can choose the school they believe best suited to the particular interests and aptitudes of their children.
>
> (DFE 1992: 10)

The emphasis here is on choice rather than selection, but none of the government's rhetoric recognises the reality of what happens, either overtly or covertly, when schools are massively oversubscribed. Yet, the White Paper goes on to say that

> The Government is committed to parity of esteem between academic, technological and creative skills, with all children – whatever their aptitude and in whatever type of school – being taught the National Curriculum to the same high standards. The Government wants to ensure that there are no tiers of schools within the maintained system [*sic*] but rather parity of esteem between different schools, in order to offer parents a wealth of choice.
>
> (DFE 1992: 10)

The impression given is that each school is to be judged on its merits, rather than as embodying the characteristics of a hierarchically arranged series of 'types'. Yet we saw earlier that parents choosing CTCs are frequently concerned with the extent to which this 'new choice of school' is similar to independent and grammar schools and different from mainstream comprehensive schools. Furthermore, looking at the reality of those reforms that have already taken place, Walford and Miller (1991) claim that, while comprehensive schools attempted to overcome the historic links between diversity of provision and inequalities of class and gender, 'City Technology Colleges have played a major part in re-legitimizing inequality of provision for different pupils'. Indeed, they argue that the 'inevitable result' of the concept of CTCs, especially when coupled with grant-maintained schools and LMS, is 'a hierarchy of schools with the private sector at the head, the CTCs and GMSs next, and the various locally managed LEA schools following' (Walford and Miller 1991: 165). While in chapter 6, we expressed some doubts about where CTCs would eventually settle in this hierarchy, the idea that there will be no hierarchy of school types at all is difficult to sustain in the light of past experience.

The 1992 White Paper rejects such pessimism and dismisses the relevance of the experience of the tripartite system of the 1950s and 1960s by arguing that we now live in 'a different educational world' with the National Curriculum ensuring equality of opportunity (DFE 1992: 10). However, the particular form of national curriculum introduced by the Thatcher government, and the arrangements for testing the outcomes, are likely to arrange schools and pupils in a hierarchy through the combined effects of LMS, competition among schools for pupils and the publication of assessment scores. This will leave the most disadvantaged and demotivated pupils concentrated in schools with low aggregate test scores and declining resources and low teacher morale. Resource differences between schools will thereby increase and their capacity to deliver any curriculum adequately will vary considerably.

There is certainly little evidence yet that, taken as a whole, the Education Reform Act 1988 is helping to provide a structure that will encompass diversity and ensure equality of opportunity for all pupils. Rather, there is some evidence that its emphasis on parental choice will further disadvantage those unable to compete in the market, by increasing the differences between popular and less popular schools. This could have disastrous consequences for some sections of the predominantly working-class and black populations who inhabit the inner cities. While they never gained an equitable share of educational resources under social democratic policies, the abandonment of planning in favour of a quasi-market seems unlikely to provide a fairer outcome. Indeed, there is a real possibility that an educational underclass will emerge in Britain's inner cities.

Ball suggests that, below the various types of schools of choice that are being fostered by current policies, there is developing a third tier of '"sink" schools – those which are unpopular and undersubscribed' (Ball 1990: 91). Disparities between the resourcing of schools within the different tiers are likely to be intensified as schools become increasingly dependent on generating extra income to supplement that which comes from the state. While schools serving affluent communities will be able to raise substantial funds, the potential for fund-raising is virtually non-existent in those very schools in which public funding is being progressively reduced.

One of the results of the 'deregulation' of schooling is that the onus is increasingly on parents to make separate applications to each school. As we saw in chapter 4, the CTC policy also introduced a new mode of selection for schools, based on the criteria of motivation, commitment and aptitude, an approach which is likely to be extended if the approach of the recent White Paper is implemented. These new modes of application and selection privilege those with the system know-how, time and energy to make applications and mount a good case (Gewirtz et al. 1992). At the same time, they discriminate against those who have more pressing immediate concerns than being an educational 'consumer'. These are often the victims of the deregulation that has already affected the labour market. They are also struggling to survive in the face of decreased social support resulting from the increased residualisation of welfare. This group includes homeless families and those living in poor housing conditions; those reliant on social fund loans for essentials like cookers and beds; and those refused loans because they cannot afford to repay them. It also includes a growing sector of women on low incomes or benefits with children or with sick partners or parents but without the family support networks to fill the gap left by the contraction of the social and health services. For such victims of welfare restructuring, applying to a CTC or grant-maintained school and mounting a good case, cannot be a primary priority. Members of this group are also less likely to have the cultural resources to exercise 'choice' whether it be in education, housing or health-care.

However, the distinction between those who are privileged and those who are disadvantaged by the CTC policy and parallel 'market' initiatives would not appear to be a straightfoward middle-class/working-class or white/black one. Most of the housing reforms were aimed particularly at council house tenants, and the CTCs were to be established in inner-city areas. While detrimental to large sections of the working class, the reforms are also likely to benefit some working-class families as well as lower-middle-class ones. Similarly, we saw that the CTC policy may have attracted particular fractions of the ethnic minority population in south-east London. But, while the new policies may reflect changes in the nature of class reproduction, they do not significantly interrupt it. Indeed, in some respects, they intensify it.

Thus, whatever the intentions of their sponsors, present policies are as likely to increase structural inequalities as to challenge them, while fostering the belief that the championing of choice provides genuinely equal opportunities for all those individuals who wish to benefit from them. For those members of disadvantaged groups who are not sponsored out of schools at the bottom of the status hierarchy, either on grounds of exceptional academic ability or (as in CTCs) alternative definitions of merit, the new arrangements may just be a more sophisticated way of reproducing traditional distinctions between different types of school and between the people who attend them. They certainly seem more likely to produce greater differentiation between schools on a linear scale of quality and esteem than the positive diversity that some of their supporters hoped for. If so, the recent reforms will represent a continuity with a long history of inequality in English education chronicled by Banks in *Parity and Prestige in English Secondary Education* (Banks 1955).

It might further be argued that the existence of the national curriculum is serving to legitimise inequality of provision, by creating the impression that, whatever the other differences between schools, all have something in common. Against the case that a degree of commonality of curricular provision will ensure equality of opportunity have to be set doubts about the extent to which the current national curriculum can respond adequately to the diversity of class, race and gender encountered in urban schools. As Secada (1989: 75) points out, the knowledge content of what is distributed through the education system raises issues of equity in that it may serve the interests of some groups at the expense of others. Certainly, some ministerial interventions about the content of programmes of study for the national curriculum raise serious questions about whether the needs of all client groups are being responded to equitably at the present time (Whitty 1992: 292–300).

CONTINUITY AND CHANGE

Even if the national curriculum created by the Education Reform Act differentiates cultures on a hierarchical basis and is as much a reflection of nostalgia for an imagined national 'past' as a recipe for modernisation, it might be thought that CTCs stand outside of all this by offering an alternative conception of excellence for inner-city schools. However, we have already noted that some of the more imaginative curriculum arrangements planned in the early CTCs, including those recommended by ORT, were abandoned as it became clear that, the Education Reform Act notwithstanding, CTCs were to be as constrained as any other state-funded school by the national curriculum. In view of the CTC mission, it is particularly ironic that this should be the case when the Confederation of British Industry has argued that the National Curriculum, by seeming to re-emphasise strong boundaries between subjects, is giving 'too much importance to narrow academic knowledge and too little to the fostering of transferable skills' (Jackson 1989). CTCs are being required to adhere to the very form of curriculum that has often been seen as partly, or even largely, to blame for the decline of British industry.

CTCs, then, embody many of the contradictions that can be identified in education policy more generally. Neo-conservative and neo-liberal policies vie with each other and with the residue of the traditional social democratic approaches to educational reform. Ball sees CTCs as actually going some way towards resolving the tensions between the cultural restorationists and those who argue that education should be more closely geared to the needs of industry (Ball 1990: 129). It is also possible to read a degree of coherence into the various policies and to see them as all addressing the core problems facing the modern state. Gamble has suggested that the paradox of at one and the same time building a strong state through increased expenditure on the military and the apparatuses of law and order, while at the same time using state power to roll back state intervention from whole areas of social activity, does have a degree of consistency. This is because the state needs to protect the market from vested interests and restrictive practices and prevent the conditions in which it can flourish being subverted either from without or within (Gamble 1983).

In similar vein, Dale (1990) argues that a policy of 'conservative modernisation', which entails 'freeing individuals for economic purposes while controlling them for social purposes', was a key feature of the Thatcher government's education policy under Baker and that it is a particularly useful concept for making sense of CTCs. We would certainly argue that it is more helpful to see CTCs in these terms than as an expression of post-modernity. Although current education policies may seem to be a response to changing economic, political and cultural priorities in modern societies, it would be difficult to argue, at least in the case of Britain, that they should be read as indicating that we have entered into a qualitatively new phase of social development. Despite the development of new forms of accumulation and changes in the state's mode of regulation, together with some limited changes in patterns of social and cultural differentiation in contemporary Britain, the continuities seem just as striking as the discontinuities.

While it is easy to see why Green (1991) and other commentators regard recent policies as a first stage towards atomisation and privatisation, current education reforms still conform to Archer's definition of a modern state education system as 'a nation-wide and differentiated collection of institutions devoted to formal education, whose overall control and supervision is at least partly governmental, and whose component parts and processes are related to one another' (Archer 1984: 19).

Visions of our moving towards a post-modern education system in a post-modern society may thus be premature or a reflection of surface appearances. To regard the current espousal of heterogeneity, pluralism and local narratives as indicative of a new social order may be to mistake phenomenal forms for structural relations. Marxist critics of theories of post-modernism and post-modernity, such as Callinicos (1989), certainly take this view and reassert the primacy of class struggle. Even Harvey (1989), who accepts that significant changes are taking place within capitalism, suggests that it may be more appropriate to see post-modernist cultural forms and more flexible modes of capital accumulation more as shifts in surface appearance rather than as signs of the emergence of some entirely new post-capitalist or even post-industrial society. At the very most, the current reforms in education discussed in this book would seem to relate to a version of post-modernity that emphasises 'distinction' and 'hierarchy' within a fragmented social order (PM1), rather than one that positively celebrates 'difference' and 'heterogeneity' (PM2) (Lash 1990).

Nevertheless, for whatever reason, CTCs and other new types of schools are developing a significant market appeal. While much of this can be explained in terms of their perceived position in a developing 'pecking order' of schools, it would be unwise to interpret it all in this way. Despite the absence of a clear post-modern break within either schooling or society, the recent reforms may have been more responsive than their critics usually concede to those subtle, but none the less tangible, social and cultural shifts that have been taking place in modern societies. Certainly, a straightforward return to the old order of things would be neither feasible nor sensible. Social democratic approaches to education which continue to favour the idea of a common school are now faced with the need to respond to increasing specialisation and diversity within contemporary societies. Just as current discussions on the left about citizenship are seeking ways of 'creating unity without denying specificity' (Mouffe, quoted in Giroux 1990), so will this be a challenge for future education policies. James Donald (1990) calls for approaches which are based on 'participation and distributive justice rather than simple egalitarianism and on cultural heterogeneity rather than a shared humanity' – a project which he himself argues puts a question mark against the idea of comprehensive education. Those who oppose CTCs and the thrust of the 1992 White Paper will need to articulate alternatives that are more successful than current Labour Party policy in challenging the present government's claim that its opponents favour a 'uniformity in educational provision' that 'presupposes that children are all basically the same and that local communities have essentially the same educational needs' (DFE 1992: 3).

Notes

1 CITY TECHNOLOGY COLLEGES: THE CONCEPT AND THE CONTEXT

1 The prospectus also resembles Manpower Services Commission publications, however, in its combination of glossy presentation, highlighted headings and economy with words. In comparison with previous DES publications, it appears self-consciously modern.

2 For a fuller account of the design of the research, see Edwards *et al.* (1992b).

3 One official described them to us as 'the most crawled-over schools in the land' since Kingshurst CTC opened in 1988.

2 THE EMERGENCE OF CITY TECHNOLOGY COLLEGES

1 Quoted from Peter Wilby's 'close-up' of Baker in *Marxism Today* April 1987: 37.

2 Baker, interviewed by Matthew Parris on *Weekend World* 7 December 1986.

3 See the profiles of Brian Griffiths (currently, as Lord Griffiths, chairman of the Schools Examination and Assessment Council) in the *Sunday Times* 26 July 1987 and the *Illustrated London News* June 1988.

4 Alfred Sherman, 'Learning to grab ideas by the horns', *Guardian* 12 September 1986. Sherman was the first director of the Centre for Policy Studies, founded in 1974 by Keith Joseph and Margaret Thatcher to counter the still predominantly collectivist approach of the Conservative Party's research department. In that article and elsewhere, Sherman emphasises the key role of the Centre in transforming the Conservatives from the 'stupid party' to one with a keen interest in theory.

5 'Plans for an independent schools network laid' was a *Guardian* headline on 19 July 1985. On 24 February 1986 it predicted the 'return of direct grant schools'.

6 The No Turning Back group's members included several future education ministers (Angela Rumbold, Michael Fallon and Eric Forth). Their 1985 pamphlet *Save Our Schools* argued for a system composed entirely of 'independent' schools, and it was this objective which the group urged on Mrs Thatcher at a Downing Street meeting the following year.

7 Boyson made this proposal in a speech to the National Council for Educational Standards on 26 April 1982.

8 In his autobiography, Young describes a visit to ORT schools in Israel in 1975 as having 'changed my life' because he saw how successful a vocationally oriented secondary education could be (Young 1990: 23). Sir Keith Joseph was also a patron of ORT.

3 RESISTANCE AND ADAPTATION

1 Noble (1992: 10) suggests that some of the corporate sponsors of President Bush's New American Schools initiative were motivated by a desire to boost their tarnished image. Some parallels between CTCs and New American schools are outlined in chapter 7.

2 For example, Ian Nash, 'Still struggling to change out of first gear', *Times Educational Supplement* 14 October 1988; R. Waterhouse, 'Mounting costs of Baker's beacons', *The Independent* 29 June 1989; S. Bates, 'Reluctant firms sealed CTCs' fate', *Guardian* 17 November 1990.

3 Address to the Teesside Junior Chamber of Commerce, 14 March 1987. At the time, Alistair Graham's consistently expressed opinion, as director of the Industrial Society, was that the government had foolishly ignored existing schools–industry links, concentrated undue attention on a few schools, and made an inappropriate request to industry to meet some of the capital needs of state education.

4 The run-down state of school buildings, especially of secondary schools, was commented on in three successive annual reports by HM Senior Chief Inspector of Schools for the school years 1987–90.

5 CTC Trust, Revenue Funding Group (undated).

4 CHOOSERS AND CHOSEN

1 Rhodes Boyson, quoted in article by T. Albert, *Guardian* 23 November 1982. When he reviewed our book on the Assisted Places Scheme (Edwards *et al.* 1989) in the *Times Higher Educational Supplement* 18 May 1990, Boyson's own conclusion was that the scheme had concentrated unduly on a fortunate few.

2 The catchment area for the John Cabot CTC, opening in Kingswood on the outskirts of Bristol in 1993, includes virtually all of the Bristol metropolitan area.

3 The figures are taken from *Parental Awareness of School Education*

(April–July 1989), a report prepared for the DES by Public Attitude Surveys Ltd and published in November of that year.

4 Personal communication from Geoffrey Walford, based on further information from his Kingshurst study.

5 David Smith, headmaster of Bradford Grammar School, in the journal *Conference* June 1987.

6 'Secondary Intake Analysis for Wandsworth Schools', September 1991, prepared by Research and Evaluation Unit, Education Department, Wandsworth Borough Council, 14 May 1992. We are grateful to Stephen Ball for this information.

5 CENTRES OF INNOVATION?

1 John MacGregor, then Secretary of State for Education, introducing the prospectus celebrating the official opening of Dixon's CTC in Bradford on 31 October 1990.

2 Lyndon Jones, principal of Harris CTC, in a letter to the *Times Educational Supplement* 13 November 1989; John Lewis, principal of Dixon's CTC, writing in its prospectus.

3 DES press notice 250/89. In the 1992 assignment of responsibilities, CTCs are grouped with grant-maintained schools in the brief of the Minister of State (Baroness Blatch), DES press office 15 April 1992.

4 'Baker scores a triumph with CTC appointment' was the *Times Educational Supplement* headline 10 September 1988.

5 Donald Naismith, director of education for Wandsworth, is a governor of ADT but not as an LEA representative. He is also on the Council of the CTC Trust.

6 For example, 'CTC staff's no-strike agreement angers unions', *Times Educational Supplement* 25 August 1989; National Union of Teachers (1989: 9).

7 One CTC we visited had an industrial plastics-moulding machine, a gift from a local firm with a vested interest in developing quite specific employment skills. It had not been used, and we observed no similar example of such directly self-interested sponsorship.

6 DISTURBING THE SYSTEM?

1 Baker, interviewed by Matthew Parris on *Weekend World* 7 December 1986.

2 Provisional figures given in a parliamentary reply to Joan Ruddock, MP, on 19 July 1991 indicated that, although Haberdashers' would meet its full capacity target of 1,100 pupils in 1991–2, it would receive £3,812 per pupil in that year rather than the £3,657 implied by the formula.

3 'Eggar launches £25 million "Technology Schools" Plan', DES press notice 414/91, 4 December 1991.

4 Edward Lister, chair of Education in Wandsworth, interviewed on

BBC TV's *On the Record*, 3 February 1992. It was pointed out that the LEA's investment in making Battersea Park School into a selective technology college would be ten times the £250,000 ceiling per school in the Technology Schools Initiative.

7 NEW SCHOOLS FOR NEW TIMES?

1 A further and inauspicious parallel with CTCs lay in the apparent reluctance of corporate sponsors to produce more than a quarter of the expected $200 million contribution towards the design costs of the projects (*Times Educational Supplement* 14 August 1992).
2 'For tomorrow's students, the next generation, we must create a New Generation of American Schools', George Bush, 18 April 1991. Brochure from New American Schools Development Corporation.

Bibliography

Adler, M., Petch, A. and Tweedie, J. (1989) *Parental Choice and Educational Policy*, Edinburgh: Edinburgh University Press.

Ainley, P. and Corney, M. (1990) *Training for the Future: The Rise and Fall of the Manpower Services Commission*, London: Cassell.

Allen, J. (1992) 'Post-industrialism and post-Fordism', in S. Hall, D. Held and T. McGrew (eds) *Modernity and its Futures*, Cambridge: Polity Press.

Andrews, M. (1991) *Time Management*, Nottingham: Djanogly CTC.

Archer, M. (1984) *Social Origins of Educational Systems*, London: Sage.

Association for Science Education (1986) *City Technology Colleges: Some Important Issues*, London: ASE.

Association of Metropolitan Authorities (1987) *City Technology Colleges*, London: AMA.

Ashworth, J., Papps, I. and Thomas, B. (1988) *Increased Parental Choice: An Economic Analysis of Some Alternative Methods of Management and Finance of Education*, Warlingham: IEA Education Unit.

Ball, S. (1990) *Politics and Policy Making: Explorations in Policy Sociology*, London: Routledge.

Ball, S. and Bowe, R. (1991) 'Micropolitics of radical change: budgets, management and control in British schools', in J. Blase (ed.) *The Politics of Life in Schools*, London: Sage.

Banks, O. (1955) *Parity and Prestige in English Secondary Education*, London: Routledge.

Barnett, C. (1986) *The Audit of War*, London: Macmillan.

Benn, C. (1987) 'Baker's dozen: city technology colleges', *Teaching London Kids* 25: 9–11.

—— (1990) 'The public price of private education and privatization', *Forum* 32, 3: 68–73.

Beresford, P. (1990) *Sunday Times Book of the Rich*, London: Sunday Times.

Blank, R. (1990) 'Educational effects of magnet schools', in W. Clune and J. Witte (eds) *Choice and Control in American Education, Vol. 2*, London and New York: Falmer Press.

Bowles, S. and Gintis, H. (1976) *Schooling in Capitalist America*, New York: Basic Books.

Boyne, R. and Rattansi, A. (eds) (1990) *Postmodernism and Society*, London: Macmillan.

Boyson, R. (1975) 'The developing case for the educational voucher', in C.B. Cox and R. Boyson (eds) *The Fight for Education*, London: Dent.

Callinicos, A. (1989) *Against Post-modernism: A Marxist Critique*, Cambridge: Polity Press.

Chitty, C. (1987) 'The commodification of education', *Forum* 29, 3: 66–9.

—— (1989) 'CTCs: a strategy for elitism', *Forum* 31, 2: 37–40.

Chubb, M. and Moe, T. (1990) *Politics, Markets and America's Schools*, Washington, DC: Brookings Institution.

—— (1992) 'Classroom revolution', *Sunday Times* 19 February, pp. 18–36.

City Technology College Trust (1991a) *A Good Education with Vocational Relevance*, London: CTC Trust.

—— (1991b) *The City and Guilds Technological Baccalaureate*, London: CTC Trust.

City Technology College Trust, Revenue Funding Group (undated) *CTCs: Recurrent Cost Comparisons*, London: CTC Trust.

Coldron, J. and Boulton, P. (1991) 'Happiness as a criterion of parents' choice of school', *Journal of Education Policy* 6, 2: 169–78.

Confederation of British Industry (CBI) (1988) *Business in Education*, London: CBI.

Cooper, B. (1987) *Magnet Schools*, Warlingham: IEA Education Unit.

Cox, C.B. and Boyson, R. (eds) (1975) *The Fight for Education: Black Paper 1975*, London: Dent.

—— (eds) (1977) *Black Paper 1977*, London: Temple.

Dale, R. (1989) *The State and Education Policy*, Milton Keynes: Open University Press.

—— (1990) 'The Thatcherite project in education: the case of the city technology colleges', *Critical Social Policy* 9, 3: 4–19.

—— (1992) 'National reform, economic crisis and "New Right" theory: a New Zealand perspective', paper presented at the American Educational Research Association annual meeting, San Francisco, 20–4 April.

Dale, R., Bowe, R., Harris, D., Loveys, M., Moore, R., Shilling, C., Sikes, P., Trevitt, J. and Valsecchi, V. (1990) *The TVEI Story: Policy, Practice and Preparation for the Workforce*, Milton Keynes: Open University Press.

Dean, C. (1990) 'Baker offspring are dear to rear', *Times Educational Supplement* 1 June.

Deem, R. and Wilkins, J. (1992) 'Governing and managing schools after the Reform Act: the LEA experience and the GMS alternative', in L. Ellison, V. Garrett and T. Simpkins (eds) *Implementing Educational Reforms: The Early Lessons*, London: Longman.

Denholm, L. (1990a) *A National Asset: Benefits and Potential of the CTCs*, Nottingham: Djanogly CTC.

—— (1990b) *Information Technology*, London: CTC Trust.

—— (1991) 'Curriculum and resources: a basis for IT provision in a CTC', CTC discussion paper.

Department of Education and Science (DES) (1986) *A New Choice of School*, London: DES.

—— (1991) *The City Technology College Kingshurst, Solihull: A Report by HMI*, London: DES.

Department for Education (DFE) (1992) *Choice and Diversity: A New Framework for Schools*, London: HMSO.

Donald, J. (1990) 'Interesting times', *Critical Social Policy* 9, 3: 39–55.

Edwards, T. (1992) *Uncertain Knowledge and Indeterminate Practice* (1991 Lawrence Stenhouse Memorial Lecture), Norwich: University of East Anglia.

Edwards, T. and Whitty, G. (1992) 'Parental choice and educational reform in Britain and the United States', *British Journal of Educational Studies* 40, 2: 101–17.

Edwards, T., Fitz, J. and Whitty, G. (1989) *The State and Private Education: An Evaluation of the Assisted Places Scheme*, Lewes: Falmer.

Edwards, T., Gewirtz, S. and Whitty, G. (1992a) 'Whose choice of schools?', in M. Arnot and L. Barton (eds) *Voicing Concerns: Sociological Perspectives on Contemporary Educational Reforms*, Wallingford: Triangle Books.

—— (1992b) 'Researching a policy in progress: the city technology college initiative', *Research Papers in Education* 7, 1: 79–104.

Fey, S. (1989) *CTC Post-16 Provision*, London: CTC Trust.

—— (1991) *CTC Characteristics: A Discussion Document*, London: CTC Trust.

Finegold, D., Keep, E., Miliband, D., Raffe, D., Spours, K., and Young, M. (1990) *A British Baccalaureat: Ending the Division betwen Education and Training*, London: Institute for Public Policy Research.

Fisher, P. (1990) *Education 2000: Educational Change with Consent*, London: Cassell.

Fitz, J., Edwards, T. and Whitty, G. (1986) 'Beneficiaries, benefits and costs: an investigation of the Assisted Places Scheme', *Research Papers in Education* 1, 3: 169–93.

Flax, J. (1987) 'Post-modernism and gender relations in feminist theory', *Signs* 12, 4: 621–43.

Forrest, R. and Murie, A. (1988) 'The social division of housing subsidies', *Critical Social Policy* 8, 2: 83–93.

Fullan, M. (1991) *The New Meaning of Educational Change*, London: Cassell.

—— (1992) *Successful School Improvement*, Milton Keynes: Open University Press.

Gamble, A. (1983) 'Thatcherism and Conservative politics', in S. Hall and M. Jacques (eds) *The Politics of Thatcherism*, London: Lawrence & Wishart.

Gewirtz, S., Walford, G. and Miller, H. (1991) 'Parents' individualist and collectivist strategies', *International Studies in Sociology of Education* 1, 1: 173–91.

Gewirtz, S., Ball, S. and Bowe, R. (1992) 'Parents, privilege and the educational marketplace', paper presented at the British Educational Research Association annual conference, Stirling University, 31 August.

Gillman, E. (1990/1) *Learning and Teaching Styles: Professional Development*, London: CTC Trust.

Giroux, H. (ed.) (1990) *Post-Modernity, Feminism and Cultural Politics*, New York: State University of New York Press.

Glazier, J. (1986) 'CTCs – so what's new?', *Education* 5 December: 488.

Glenn, C. (1988) *The Myth of the Common School*. Amherst, Mass.: University of Massachusetts Press.

Gordon, L. (1992) 'The New Zealand state and educational reforms: "competing" interests', paper presented at the American Educational Research Association annual meeting, San Francisco, 20–4 April.

Grace, G. (1991) 'Welfare Labourism versus the New Right', *International Studies in the Sociology of Education* 1, 1: 37–48.

Green, A. (1991) 'The peculiarities of English education', in Education Group II, *Education Limited: Schooling and Training and the New Right since 1979*, London: Unwin Hyman.

Hagen, S. (1992) *The Foreign Language Needs of British Business: A CTC Response*, London: CTC Trust.

Halpin, D., Power, S. and Fitz, J. (1991) 'Grant-maintained schools: making a difference without being different', *British Journal of Educational Studies* 39, 4: 409–24.

—— (1992) 'Opting for self-governance: change and continuity in grant-maintained schools', in L. Ellison, V. Garrett and T. Simkins (eds) *Implementing Educational Reform: The Early Lessons*, London: Longman.

Halsey, A., Heath, A. and Ridge, J. (1980) *Origins and Destinations: Family, Class and Education in Modern Britain*, Oxford: Clarendon Press.

Hammer, M. and Flude, M. (1989) 'Grant-maintained schools are nothing to do with party politics: an interview with Andrew Turner, director of the Grant Maintained Schools Trust', *Journal of Education Policy* 4, 4: 373–85.

Harris, R. (1969) 'The larger lessons of Enfield', in C.B. Cox and A. Dyson (eds) *Black Paper Two: The Crisis in Education*, London: Critical Quarterly Society.

Harris, R. and Seldon, A. (1979) *Over-ruled on Welfare*, London: Institute of Economic Affairs.

Harvey, D. (1989) *The Condition of Postmodernity: An Enquiry into the Origins of Cultural Change*, Oxford: Basil Blackwell.

Haviland, J. (ed.) (1988) *Take Care, Mr Baker*, London: Fourth Estate.

Heath, A. (1980) 'Class and meritocracy in British education', in A. Finch and P. Scrimshaw (eds) *Standards, Schooling and Education*, London: Hodder & Stoughton.

Hennessy, P. (1990) *Whitehall*, London: Fontana.

Her Majesty's Inspectororate of Schools (HMI) (1992) *The Technical and Vocational Initiative in England and Wales 1983–91*, London: DES.

Hess, A. (1990) *Chicago School Reform: How it is and How it Came to Be*, Chicago: Panel on Public School Policy and Finance.

Hillgate Group (1986) *Whose Schools? A Radical Manifesto*, London: Claridge Press.

—— (1987) *The Reform of British Education*, London: Claridge Press.

ILEA (1984) *Improving Secondary Schools*, Hargreaves Report, London: Inner London Education Authority.

Jackson, M. (1989) 'CBI struggles to "save" curriculum from Baker', *Times Educational Supplement*, 24 March.

Jamieson, I. (1986) 'Corporate hegemony or pedagogic liberation: the schools–industry movement in England and Wales', in R. Dale (ed.) *Education, Training and Employment: Towards a New Vocationalism*, London: Pergamon.

Jessop, B., Bonnett, K., Bromley, S. and Ling, T. (1987) 'Popular capitalism, flexible accumulation and left strategy', *New Left Review* 165: 104–23.

Jessup, G. (1991) *Outcomes: NVQs and the Emerging Model of Education and Training*, Lewes: Falmer Press.

Johnson, N. (1990) *Reconstructing the Welfare State: A Decade of Change 1980–90*, Hertfordshire: Harvester Wheatsheaf.

Jones, R. (1990) 'Post-16 education', paper to CTC Trust Curriculum Development Steering Committee, November.

—— (1992) *Post-16 Provision in CTCs: Bridging the Divide*, London: CTC Trust.

Kenway, J. (1992) 'Marketing education in the postmodern age', paper presented at the American Educational Research Association annual meeting, San Francisco, 20–4 April.

Knight, C. (1990) *The Making of Tory Education Policy in Post-War Britain 1950–1986*, Lewes: Falmer Press.

Lash, S. (1991) *Sociology of Postmodernism*, London: Routledge.

Le Grand, J. (1991) 'Quasi-markets and social policy', *Economic Journal* 101: 1256–67.

—— (1992) 'Paying for or providing welfare?', paper presented at the Social Policy Association annual conference, Nottingham University, July.

Louis, K.S. and Miles, M. (1992) *Improving the Urban High School*, London: Cassell.

Lynch, I. (1991) *Electronic Registration and Recording Achievement*, London: CTC Trust.

Lyotard, J.F. (1986) *The Postmodern Condition*, Manchester: Manchester University Press.

McCulloch, G. (1989a) 'CTCs: a new choice of school?', *British Journal of Educational Studies* 37, 1: 30–43.

—— (1989b) *The Secondary Technical School: A Usable Past?*, Lewes: Falmer Press.

McLeod, J. (1988) 'CTCs: a study of the character and progress of an educational reform', *Local Government Studies* January/February: 75–82.

Mathieson, M. and Bernbaum, G. (1988) 'The British disease: a British tradition?', *British Journal of Educational Studies* 36: 126–74.

Metz, M. (1990) 'Potentialities and problems of choice in desegregation plans', in W. Clune and J. Witte (eds) *Choice and Control in American Education, Vol. 1*, London and New York: Falmer Press.

Moon, B. (1983) *Comprehensive Schools: Challenge and Change*, Windsor: NFER Nelson.

Morrell, F. (1989) *Children of the Future*, London: Hogarth Press.

Murphy, R., Brown, P. and Partington, J. (1990) *An Evaluation of the Effectiveness of City Technology Colleges' Selection Procedures*, report to the DES (May).

National Union of Teachers (NUT) (1989) *City Technology Colleges: No Thanks!*, London: NUT.

Naylor, F. (1985) *Technical Schools: A Tale of Four Countries*, London: Centre for Policy Studies.

Noble, D. (1992) 'New American schools and the new world order', paper presented at the American Educational Research Association annual meeting, San Francisco, 20–4 April.

O'Connor, M. (1986) 'Cuckoos in the nest', *Guardian* 18 November.

Office of Population Censuses and Surveys (OPCS) (1980) *Classification of Occupations 1980*, London: HMSO.

O'Hear, A. (1987) 'The importance of traditional learning', *British Journal of Educational Studies* 35, 2: 102–14.

—— (1991) *Education and Democracy: Against the Educational Establishment*, London: Claridge Press.

Ouston, J. (1990) *The Evaluation of Education 2000: The Hertfordshire Project*, final report to the DES (autumn).

Ozga, J. (1990) 'Policy research and policy theory', *Journal of Education Policy* 5, 4: 359–63.

Phillips, M. (1988) 'Why black people are backing Baker', *Guardian* 9 September.

Prais, S. and Wagner, K. (1986) 'Schooling standards in England and Germany: some summary comparisons bearing on economic performance', *Compare* 16: 5–36.

Pring, R. (1987) 'Privatization in education', *Journal of Education Policy* 2, 4: 289–99.

Regan, D. (1990) *City Technology Colleges: Potentialities and Perils*, London: Centre for Policy Studies.

Riddell, P. (1992) 'Is it the end of politics?', *The Times* 3 August.

Robins, K. (1991) 'Tradition and translation: national culture in its global context', in J. Corner and S. Harvey (eds) *Enterprise and Heritage: Crosscurrents of National Culture*, London: Routledge.

Rogers, R. (1991) 'A break with house style', *Times Educational Supplement* 21 June: 26–7.

Rowan, P. (1988) 'The huge gap between reality and rhetoric', *Times Educational Supplement* 25 November.

Rustin, M. (1989) 'The politics of post-Fordism: or, the trouble with "New Times"', *New Left Review* 175: 54–79.

Secada, W. (ed.) (1989) *Equity in Education*, Lewes and Philadelphia: Falmer Press.

Seldon, A. (1986) *The Riddle of the Voucher*, London: Institute of Economic Affairs.

Sexton, S. (1986) 'Schools: still the parents wait', *The Times* 13 August.

—— (1987) *Our Schools: A Radical Policy*, Warlingham: Institute of Economic Affairs Education Unit.

Shilling, C. (1987) 'Work experience and schools: factors influencing the participation of industry', *Journal of Education Policy* 2, 2: 131–47.

Simon, B. (1987) 'Lessons in elitism', *Marxism Today* (September), reprinted in Simon (1992).

—— (1992) *What Future for Education?*, London: Lawrence & Wishart.

Slater, S. (1987) 'Delivering the goods: education and industry – a partnership in action', *School Organisation* 7, 1: 35–8.

—— (1988) 'Industrial links', in D. Warwick (ed.) *Teaching and Learning through Modules*, Oxford: Basil Blackwell.

Smithers, A. and Robinson, P. (1991) *Beyond Compulsory Schooling: A Numerical Picture*, London: Council for Industry and Higher Education.

Taylor, C. (1986) *Employment Examined*, London: Centre for Policy Studies.

—— (1987) 'Qualifying pupils for the year 2000', *Daily Telegraph* 17 August.

—— (1990) *Raising Educational Standards*, London: Centre for Policy Studies.

Thompson, K. (1992) 'Social pluralism and post-modernity', in S. Hall, D. Held and T. McGrew (eds) *Modernity and its Futures*, Cambridge: Polity Press.

Walford, G. (1990), *Privatization and Privilege in Education*, London: Routledge.

—— (1991a) 'City technology colleges: a private magnetism?', in G. Walford (ed.) *Private Schooling: Tradition, Change and Diversity*, London: Paul Chapman.

—— (1991b) 'Choice of school at the first CTC', *Educational Studies* 17, 1: 65–75.

Walford, G. and Miller, H. (1991) *City Technology College*, Milton Keynes: Open University Press.

Watkins, P. (1991) *Knowledge and Control in the Flexible Workplace*, Geelong: Deakin University Press.

West, E.G. (1982) 'Education vouchers: evolution or revolution?', *Economic Affairs* October: 14–19.

Whitty, G. (1990) 'The politics of the Education Reform Act', in P. Dunleavy, A. Gamble and G. Peel (eds) *Developments in British Politics: 3*, London: Macmillan.

—— (1992) 'Education, economy and national culture', in R. Bocock and K. Thompson (eds) *Social and Cultural Forms of Modernity*, Cambridge: Polity Press.

Whitty, G. and Edwards, T. (1992) 'School choice in Britain and the USA: their origins and significance', paper presented at the American Educational Research Association annual meeting, San Francisco, 20–4 April.

Whitty, G. and Menter, I. (1991) 'The progress of restructuring', in D. Coulby and L. Bash (eds) *Contradiction and Conflict in Education*, London: Cassell.

Young, D. (Lord) (1990) *The Enterprise Years: A Businessman in the Cabinet*, London: Headline.

Index